The FLOWER ARRANGING EXPERT

Dr. D.G.Hessayon

All Editions & Reprints: 320,000 copies

Published by Expert Books
a division of Transworld Publishers

A catalogue record for this book is available from the British Library

TRANSWORLD PUBLISHERS
61-63 Uxbridge Road, London W5 5SA
a division of the Random House Group Ltd

Distributed in the United States
by Sterling Publishing Co. Inc.,
387 Park Avenue South,
New York,
NY 10016-8810

EXPERT BOOKS

Contents

Reproduction by Spot On Digital Imaging Ltd., Milton Court, Gomm Road, High Wycombe, Bucks., HP13 7DJ
Printed and bound by Mohn Media Mohndruck GmbH

ISBN 0 903505 41 X　　　　© D. G. HESSAYON 2003

CHAPTER 1

INTRODUCTION

If you cut an assortment of flowers and leafy stems from the garden and put them into a water-filled jug or vase, you will have made a flower arrangement. Some of the plant material may be quite unsuitable and will quickly die, the colours may clash and the overall effect may be a mess, but it *is* an arrangement.

The purpose of this book is to show you how to do better. It will help you to choose the right sort of flowers and foliage, and tell you how to prepare ('condition') them before making an arrangement. It also talks about the things you will need to buy and the proper way to keep the plant material in place in the container.

This is the craft side of flower arranging, and as with all crafts there are a number of rules to learn. Things are a little different when we turn to the artistic side of the operation — the creation of the floral design, which simply means the way we group the plant material together. Here there is disagreement among the experts over the question of the need for clear-cut rules. A growing number of arrangers belong to the Natural school which believes that the flowers and stems should be grouped informally to give a 'straight-from-the-garden' look. No rule books for these arrangers — just a keen artistic eye, simple containers, and a collection of garden, shop-bought and/or country-side flowers. The Formal school sees things differently — for them the floral arrangement is a stylised affair with a distinct geometric shape. There is no question of following your own instincts here — each one of the many modern styles (Symmetrical triangle, Inverted crescent, Hogarth curve etc) involves clear-cut rules. Finally there is the Modern school, which creates shapes that are neither as nature intended nor is there any trace of formality.

So what are you to do? Should you forget all about the rules of design set out in Chapter 3 and become a 'natural' flower arranger, or should you stick slavishly to the concepts and rules of the 'Line-mass' styles which were so dominant in home flower arranging until recently?

The best plan is to take a middle course. Get to know and try out the basic rules concerning colour, shape, proportion, texture and so on as described on later pages, and then adapt them or even ignore them to suit your own taste and artistic talent. How far you move away from the shapes of traditional floral design will depend to some extent on why you have decided to make a flower arrangement.

Maybe you are creating the display to satisfy a desire 'to make something' and at the same time to create a feature which will brighten up a spot in the house — a bare shelf, an occasional table, an empty fireplace etc. Here you should set out to produce something which really pleases *you*. It may be a geometric shape, a bunch of wild flowers in a jug or a complex abstract arrangement, but it only has to please you so this is the time to experiment.

The second possible reason for making an arrangement is to create a display which is designed to please others — the table display for a dinner party, the decoration for a church festival, the wedding floral display and so on. Here we often incorporate more eye-catching material (Orchids, Lilies etc) than we would use in the ordinary home display and the style chosen is usually one of the formal geometric ones described in Chapter 3.

The third motive for making an arrangement is money, and this takes us into the world of the florist and the professional floral decorator. It is essential to understand at the outset that the florist is not simply a flower arranger with extra skills and artistry — there are some poor florists and many extremely fine flower arrangers. The difference is one of approach — the floral decorator must produce a display which is eye-catching and which the customers feel they could not have done for themselves. There is no room here for homely touches — one of our greatest floral decorators once wrote that the worst insult which could be paid to one of his creations would be to have it described as 'nice'. So the professional generally uses more flowers and less foliage than the amateur, and techniques such as wiring and tying are employed.

The final reason for making a flower arrangement is to try to win a prize at a local or national show. Here the rule book is all-important — the show schedule clearly sets out the type of design to be created, and to ignore any one of the requirements may result in N.A.S. (Not According to Schedule) on your card.

So far we have been talking about fresh plant material cut from the garden or bought from a shop, but longer-lasting displays can be created with home-prepared or shop-bought dried flowers. These days there is also a wide range of artificial material available — the silk and plastic which may be hated by the purist but with a role to play where permanence is all-important.

This book can teach you much, especially if you are a beginner, but it cannot turn you into a floral artist. In the pages which follow you will find many styles and techniques, and by following the step-by-step instructions you should be able to make attractive displays which your family and friends will admire. Artistry, however, is a talent within you and is not to be found in a book.

The encouraging point is that many people discover that they do have a latent artistic talent for flower arranging which comes to the fore once they have learnt the basic guidelines. For them the world of stunning displays and Free-style arrangements opens up and so does an all-absorbing hobby. Maybe that won't happen to you, but you *can* produce arrangements which will be good enough to qualify you as an expert flower arranger. Read on and learn the secrets.

THE SIX STEPS TO SUCCESS

STEP 1 Read the following pages carefully. Some of the basics will probably be well-known to you, but there may be styles, techniques and plants which are new.

STEP 2 Buy the equipment and mechanics recommended as essential on pages 6–9. Obtain a small range of containers — you will not need many at this stage. Fortunately the hardware required for flower arranging is much less expensive than even the simplest tools needed for outdoor gardening.

STEP 3 Try out some of the styles illustrated in Chapter 3 — follow the procedures set out in Chapter 4 to make the arrangement. It is a good idea at this stage to follow a few of the precise step-by-step recipes to be found in nearly all books on flower arranging. Alternatively you can try to reproduce an attractive display illustrated in a magazine. This step is no more 'artistically creative' than painting by numbers, but it will give a rewarding result and build up your confidence.

STEP 4 Now try to create a few of your own arrangements, using the basic rules for conditioning and arranging but with your own choice of plants and designs. At this stage there is no need to spend a great deal on shop-bought flowers — you can learn all the principles of design by using garden flowers, stems cut from shrubs and trees, and material gathered from the countryside. Be responsible when gathering wild flowers — see Chapter 11.

STEP 5 Look at arrangements in hotels, florists, flower shows, churches etc as the time has come for you to try more ambitious arrangements. With the skills you have now learnt and with some dramatic flowers from the florist see if you can create a well-balanced and truly bold display. At this stage you will probably have to buy some of the optional extras listed on pages 6–9.

STEP 6 If the flower arranging bug has really bitten you then join a flower arranging club. Enter your displays at the local shows ... and clear a shelf for your cups!

BUYING CUT FLOWERS : HOW WE COMPARE

Amount spent per person each year : Top nation = 100

SWITZERLAND	100
NORWAY	78
ITALY	64
JAPAN	60
GERMANY	55
AUSTRIA	52
SWEDEN	51
HOLLAND	49
BELGIUM	44
DENMARK	40
FRANCE	38
UNITED STATES	31
UNITED KINGDOM	25
GREECE	21
SPAIN	18

Source: Flower Council of Holland

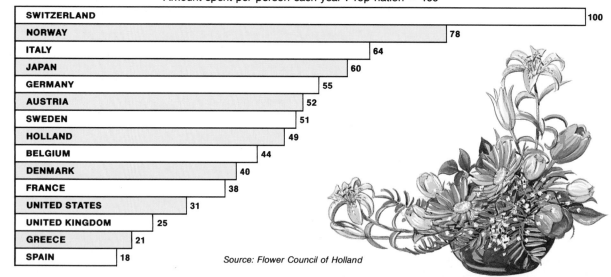

CHAPTER 2
THE BASIC INGREDIENTS

CONTAINER
A receptacle which holds the arrangement — it may or may not be hidden by the plant material. The container must be waterproof if fresh flowers and/or foliage are used
See pages 10–11

BASE
An item which is placed underneath the container to protect the surface of the support and/or to add to the beauty of the display
See page 12

ACCESSORY
An item of non-plant material which is included within or alongside an arrangement. Its role may be functional (e.g a candle) or decorative (e.g a figurine)
See page 13

EQUIPMENT
A tool or other aid used to ensure that a satisfactory arrangement of the plant material is created within the container
See pages 8–9

MECHANICS
Items used to keep the flowers, foliage and stems in place within the container. The most popular type is floral foam — the other two important ones are the pinholder and chicken wire
See pages 6–7

PLANT MATERIAL
A large group of items including flowers, foliage, stems, fruits, seed-heads, fungi, moss, wood, vegetables and berries. These materials may be fresh, dried or artificial
See pages 14–17

SUPPORT
The structure on which the container stands. With the exception of fireplace displays, arrangements are rarely placed at ground level — the usual supports in the home are tables, sideboards, alcoves and shelves. The best support for an all-round triangular arrangement is a **pedestal** made of wood, stone or metal. The usual height is about 3 ft (1 m). The pedestal display is generally associated with large arrangements in churches, stately homes etc, but more modest ones do have a place in the home

Mechanics

Placing flowers in a vase or jug of water is an age-old way of creating a floral display, but for nearly all modern-day arrangements it is necessary to use materials which keep the foliage and flowers in place within the container. These materials and their associated aids are known as mechanics. They must be fixed securely and should be hidden from view. Only a few (floral foam, adhesive clay and frogs) are essential items for the beginner — the rest are optional extras.

ADHESIVE TAPE
(Other name : 'Oasis Tape')

This strong sticky tape is available in both wide and narrow forms. The wide tape is mainly used to secure floral foam or crumpled chicken wire to the container. Narrow tape is occasionally stretched across the top of a shallow wide-mouthed container in criss-cross fashion to form a plant-holding grid

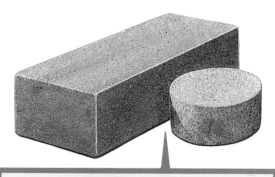

FLORAL FOAM
(Other name : 'Oasis')

Usually referred to by its most popular brand name, this cellular plastic material was invented in the 1940s and has become the leading mechanic for the home flower arrangement. There are two types — green foam which is soaked in water and then used for fresh plant material, and brown or grey foam which is used only for dry and artificial displays. The green foam can be bought in various shapes — 'blocks' and 'rounds' are the most popular. It is extremely light, but the weight increases by over 30 times when saturated. This green foam should never be allowed to dry out once it has been soaked — if you wrap it in foil or plastic film after use it should be suitable for several more arrangements. The great advantage of foam is that stems can be held at any angle in both shallow and deep containers, and the problem of smelly water is removed. Just a few drawbacks — extra support with chicken wire is necessary for a large display and a few plants (e.g Daffodils and Tulips) find water uptake difficult. See Chapter 4 for details on how to use floral foam for securing fresh plant material

FROG

This is the simplest type of foam anchor. It is a small plastic disc with 4 vertical prongs — the base is attached to the container with adhesive clay and the block or round of floral foam is pressed down on to the prongs. More than one may be required if a large block of floral foam is used

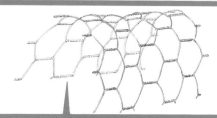

CHICKEN WIRE
(Other names : Wire mesh, Wire netting)

The grade to buy is fine gauge 2 in. (5 cm) mesh. Cut off the firm edge, roll into a tube, crumple into a ball and fit into the container — see Chapter 4 for details. Chicken wire is the preferred mechanic for an arrangement with a large number of tall or heavy stems. The 1 in. mesh grade is often used to cover a floral foam block if a large display is planned. Some (but not all) experts prefer galvanised wire to the plastic-coated variety — be careful not to scratch the sides of a valuable container. Wash and dry after use — it can be used again and again

ADHESIVE CLAY
(Other name : 'Oasis Fix')

A non-setting sticky clay in strip form which holds dry surfaces together. It is widely used for securing a frog, pinholder or candle cup (see page 11) to the container — brown and green types are available. It is difficult to remove — wipe off traces with white spirit. **Plasticine** can be used as a substitute

FLORIST CONE
(Other names : Flower tube, Flower funnel)

This miniature vase is for the floral decorator rather than the home flower arranger. It is used in large arrangements where foliage or flowers need to be placed above their stem height. The usual type of cone is about 1 ft (30 cm) long and the pointed end is generally tied to a cane which is then pushed into the floral foam or chicken wire. Fill the cone with water before inserting the stems. Keep topped up

GLUE

Quick-drying glue is used in dried flower arrangements to attach flowers or leaves to the container or other plant material. When using with stalkless flowers make sure that the glue is applied to the solid base of the bloom and not just to some of the petals. The most convenient way to apply glue is through a **Glue Gun**

PEBBLES & MARBLES

Small pebbles have long been used to hold the stems of cut flowers. Round marbles or flattened glass **nuggets** in a glass vase can add to the attractiveness of the display. When inserting the stems there will be some slight movement of the arrangement — a drawback with a strictly formal display but often an advantage with an informal one

PINHOLDER
(Other name : Kenzan)

A series of sharply-pointed pins are firmly held in a solid base which may be circular or rectangular. Its main advantage is that it will hold thick and heavy stems securely — the pinholder may be used on its own in a shallow dish or with other mechanics for a large display in a deep container. Choose a model with a heavy base and a large number of sharp brass pins. The drawback with this mechanic is that it is expensive — if you can have only one then choose the 3 in. (7.5 cm) round size. Stick it to the base of the container with adhesive clay. With the **Well Pinholder** there is no need for a container as the metal dish around the pinholder holds water. See Chapter 4 for details on how to use a pinholder

SETTING CLAY
(Other name : 'Dri-Hard')

A setting clay is used as the mechanic in permanent dry and artificial flower arrangements. This material sets solid after a few hours which means that neither the clay nor the plant material is re-usable. **Plaster of Paris** is a popular alternative for securing the stems of topiary trees in pots

NON-SETTING CLAY
(Other name : 'Stay Soft')

A non-setting clay is used as the mechanic in dry and artificial flower arrangements where the plant material is to be removed and re-used at a later date or where non-permanent accessories such as candles are to be inserted. **Plasticine** can be used as an alternative

Equipment

It is important if you are a beginner not to get the wrong impression from the large array of tools and other equipment illustrated and described on these two pages. Only a few (bucket, scissors, knife and watering can) are essential items for the beginner — the rest are optional extras. Do keep the sharp things such as scissors and knives well away from children and try to store all the items together in a box. When arranging flowers place a large plastic sheet over the work surface.

PAINTS & FINISHES

Aerosol paints can be used at any time of the year but it is at Christmas that they really come into their own — arrangements with gold or silver pine-cones, berries, leaves and flowers can be seen everywhere. These spray-on paints are usually applied to dried or artificial material but can with care be sprayed on to fresh flowers and foliage. Acrylic paints can be brushed on to dried leaves and blooms, and a sealing aerosol or lacquer hair spray can be applied to a dried arrangement to prevent flowers and seed-heads from shattering. Paints are widely used, of course, on containers, mechanics, bases etc as well as on plant material

BUCKET

A water-filled bucket is a vital piece of equipment for collecting flowers from the garden and for conditioning the blooms before making an arrangement. Choose the type with side handles as the standard free-swinging handle can damage flowers during transport. Do not use the kitchen pail — keep one or more buckets just for flower arranging and keep them scrupulously clean. It is a good idea to have at least 2 buckets — a small one for short stems and a large narrow one for tall plant material

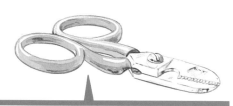

FLORAL SCISSORS

Most ordinary scissors are not suitable for cutting stems — they tend to crush the tissues. Choose a floral pair — the blades are short and one is serrated. At the base there may be a notch — use this for cutting thin wire, but not for woody stems or heavy-gauge wire. Make sure that there is plenty of room for your fingers and thumb

MISTER

A hand sprayer capable of producing a fine mist of water droplets is an aid to keeping an arrangement looking fresh in warm weather. Apply the mist slightly above the top of the display — do this once the arrangement is finished and repeat daily if you can

WIRE CUTTERS

A useful tool for heavy cutting work — this is the way to cut chicken wire, plastic stems of artificial flowers and thick stub wires

CANDLE HOLDER

Various types of plastic candle holder are available for inserting in floral foam or placing in a pinholder. Buy a metal-lined holder if the candle is to be lit rather than serve purely as decoration

TURNTABLE

This piece of equipment is by no means essential and would be a waste of money if you make facing rather than all-round arrangements (see page 19). It is a useful aid, however, if you regularly make all-round displays and is almost essential if you make them on the grand scale

WIRE

Wire is much more widely used by florists than by flower arrangers — the professional uses it to support drooping stems and for the construction of posies, corsages etc. There is still a place for wire in flower arranging, however, where it is used to make false stems for dried and artificial flowers and to bind clumps of blooms together. There are basically 3 types of wire. The strongest is **stub wire** which is bought in 5 in. (130 mm) to 18 in. (460 mm) green, blue or black lengths. The usual thickness is 18–26 gauge (1.25–0.46 mm wide). **Rose wire** is thinner — 7 in. (180 mm) lengths of 28–32 gauge (0.35–0.28 mm wide) silver wire for fine work. **Reel wire** is blue, green, silver or black and wound on a bobbin — it is extensively used by florists for binding plant material

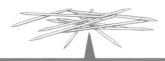

COCKTAIL STICKS
(Other name : Toothpicks)

Not in all the textbooks, but a handy multi-purpose aid. Use a cocktail stick to create a hole in floral foam for a soft stem or use one to attach a fruit to the foam holding a flower display. Several sticks are sometimes taped around the base of a candle to secure it in a table arrangement

SECATEURS

Never try to cut through thick and woody stems with ordinary scissors — use instead a pair of secateurs. You can buy the ordinary garden type, but there are narrow ones made specially for the flower arranger

CUT FLOWER PRESERVATIVE
(Other names : 'Chrysal', 'Bio Flowerlife', Cut flower food)

Several brands are available in powder or liquid form. A cut flower preservative is basically a bacteriocide to prevent slime and smells from developing in the vase-water, plus sugar to prolong the life of fresh flowers. It is worthwhile to use one of these products at the conditioning stage. A do-it-yourself recipe is 3 teaspoons of sugar and 1 drop of household bleach to each pint of water

FLORAL TAPE
(Other name : Stem-binding tape)

This ½ in. (12 mm) wide tape is bought in a roll and is used to cover artificial stems made of wire. It stretches slightly when wound round the item to be covered and sticks to itself when warmed by the hands. This tape used to be made exclusively from gutta-percha, but nowadays plastic and waxed paper are used

KNIFE

Buy a craft knife with a sharp blade — it will have all sorts of uses. You will need it for scraping stems, removing leaves and stripping away thorns. It is also employed for preparing stem ends by making a sloping cut and occasionally a vertical slit. There is also floral foam to cut and excess clay to remove

WATERING CAN

Vital, of course, for topping up the water supply in the container or floral foam holding a fresh flower arrangement. Buy a plastic one and look for 2 important features — the spout should be long and narrow, and it should arise from the base of the can

Containers

The range of containers is vast. They come in all sorts of shapes, sizes and materials — glass, pottery, metal, wood, plastic, cane, terracotta and so on. In some displays the container is covered by plant or other material — if it is not then you must make sure that it complements and does not dominate the flowers and foliage. The container, plants and the surroundings must all be right for each other — a rustic-style container in a chintzy room, a muted coloured vase against a pastel background, a tall cylinder for a stylised modern arrangement, and so on. In most instances the best choice has a matt or metallic surface in green, black, brown, cream or gold. You will need a large selection — charity shops, bring-and-buy sales etc are an excellent source.

VASE & JUG

There is no precise definition of a vase, but it is generally taken to mean a container which is at least as tall as it is wide, and is often quite narrow with a restricted mouth. It remains the favourite container for cut flowers and the choice is immense. The glass vase continues to be popular, although underwater stems can look unattractive — one answer is to partly fill the vase with glass marbles or nuggets (see page 7). A **bud vase** is a tall and thin vase which holds a single specimen of Rose, Tulip or Orchid. Metal vases were once very popular, but the Victorian **silver trumpet vase** is out of favour. Pottery and plastic now dominate the scene — remember to put a saucer or other water-holding base under an unglazed pottery or terracotta container. Do not forget the do-it-yourself vase — plastic bottles and metal tins can be turned into vases by means of plaster plus beads, shells, rope, cane etc

The vase should be in keeping with the type of display and the furnishings of the room in which it is to stand. Tall spikes of flowers generally call for a vase with near-vertical sides, and very bright surfaces or showy patterns are rarely successful. Jugs are lipped containers with a single handle — useful for old-world and 'natural' arrangements

BASKET

A popular container for dried flower arrangements — wicker and preserved plant material seem to be natural partners. Willow is the usual choice, although baskets made of bamboo, rush, grapevine and even lavender are available. Colours range from pale cream to near black, and garden centres usually offer a large selection. It is often wise to choose closely-woven wicker so that the mechanics are hidden from view, and the best selection for most purposes is a shallow and wide basket with a high handle. Once again the basic rule applies — the size chosen must be right for the amount of plant material available. For fresh flower arrangements it will be necessary to have a waterproof container within — this can be either a plastic bowl or a sheet of polythene stapled to the inner rim. A **hamper** is a square or rectangular lidded basket

WALL HANGER

The hanging **half bowl** in pottery, cane or terracotta has been available for hundreds of years. This type of container is best used with dried or artificial leaves and flowers, and the arrangement should be made on a table before hanging it on the wall. The **pew end** or **hanging frame** is different — this is a handled wire or plastic frame in which a block of moist or dry foam is inserted and then used for making a fresh or dried arrangement

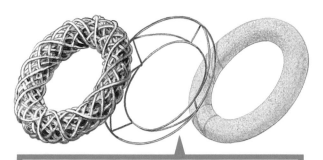

WREATH FRAME

Wreaths bedecked with seasonal flowers, berries and foliage are favourite features for the table and door at Christmas, and are popular year-round features in the U.S. The usual starting point is a shop-bought frame — choices include a woven cane ring, a wire frame in which moss is inserted, a frame covered with real or artificial conifer foliage, and a floral foam ring

CANDLE CUP

It is virtually impossible to create a worthwhile display within the confines of the cup at the top of a candlestick. The answer is the candle cup — a shallow dish of plastic or metal which holds a block or round of floral foam, and which has a short stem at the base. Fix this stem into a candlestick or bottle with adhesive clay and tape the piece of foam in place before you begin the arrangement

BOWL & TRAY

These are the shallow group of containers. The **cup** and **dish** are shallower than the **fish bowl** type, and are widely used for table arrangements. A **tazza** is a cup borne on a relatively tall and narrow stem — an **urn** is a more robust cup in pottery, stone or plastic borne on a short and stout stem and often with handles and a square base. Even more shallow is the tray — a flat container with raised sides used for dried and artificial displays and also for Line arrangements (see pages 24–27) with fresh plant material. The container without any sides is the **board** — a piece of cork, decorative wood etc on which floral foam or clay is placed and in which dried or artificial plant material is inserted

ROSE BOWL

Once a favourite container for table decoration but no longer popular. The low cylindrical base of pottery or glass holds water, and the plant-holding lid consists of either a criss-cross of thick silvered wires or a series of round holes for the stems. Useful for a posy-type arrangement

MISCELLANEOUS OBJECTS

The list of suitable household items is almost endless — jelly moulds, wine glasses, decanters, kettles, saucepans, old aerosol tops, coffee pots etc. Other objects which can serve as containers include shells and driftwood. Hollowed-out vegetable marrow and melon are eye-catching, but the gas emitted by the living container shortens the life of cut flowers

FLORAL FOAM CONTAINER

A plastic container which has internal projections designed to hold a block or round of floral foam. There is a shallow dish for green foam and cut flowers, and a tray for brown foam and dried or artificial material. This type of container is cheap but it is purely functional. This means that it should be either hidden by plant material or be placed in an attractive outer container

Bases

A base is an object placed between the container and the support on which it stands. In the home it is an optional extra, used to protect the polished surface of the support (table, shelf, bookcase etc) from water splashes and condensation. With an exhibit at a show it may well be essential as a feature of the overall design. A base is often used to link the arrangement with accessories, and it can be employed to improve both the visual appeal and sense of balance. It is, however, a common mistake to overdo it and have a base which is so large and/or bright that the eye is diverted away from the floral display.

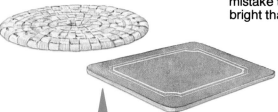

TABLE MAT

A straw, bamboo or plastic-faced table mat is the most popular base for an arrangement which is to be displayed in the home. Be careful which one you choose if it will be visible — avoid shiny and highly decorated surfaces. In most cases the table mat is not meant to add to the decorative effect, so use the smallest practical size

TREE SECTION

The crosscut of a tree trunk with or without bark makes an excellent decorative base for some but not all arrangements. An oval section is a favourite for holding containers with Landscape exhibits or Line arrangements (see Chapter 3) — the container is usually set at one side rather than in the middle of the base. The tree section can be left untreated or stained with a wood dye, and is often coated with furniture wax or varnish

WOOD BASE

Rectangles or rounds made out of plywood, blockboard, chipboard or fibreboard can all be used, but the most popular by far is the cork base. The most useful size is 1 ft (30 cm) across. Choose a colour which is in keeping with the arrangement and the surroundings

STONE BASE

Pieces of marble, slate, alabaster, limestone etc make excellent decorative bases in the right setting. Stone gives a feeling of solidity, and a section which has a hollow designed to hold a small container is especially useful

ORIENTAL BASE

Use with care. This fancy trivet-type base will heighten the 'oriental' appearance of a decorated Chinese vase with a large and exotic arrangement, but it would be quite out of place for a stylish Ikebana arrangement (see page 25) in a plain black cylinder

COVERED BASE

Plain rounds of wood are sometimes covered with felt or stretch nylon to make them more suitable as bases. The cloth is either cut and glued on to the board or tailored as an elasticated slipcover in which the board is placed. Decorative trim can be sewn around the edge, but do avoid making the cloth-covered base too ornate

Accessories

An accessory is an item of non-plant material which is included with or alongside the arrangement. Its purpose is generally purely decorative although candles which are lit serve a practical function. Some flower arrangers never use accessories except at Christmas, when bells, ribbons, candles etc are key features of wreaths and table arrangements. The situation is different for the show exhibitor — accessories are an essential feature for the displays used in interpretative classes. For example, it would be hard to think of an entry in the 'Seascape' class which did not include at least one of the following — shells, pebbles, rope, netting or a coral fan. Accessories can add interest to a home as well as a show display, but restraint is essential. Fruit, moss and driftwood are sometimes added to an arrangement, but these are items of plant material and not true accessories.

CANDLE

Candles are an important accessory for the dining table arrangement. When left unlit they provide a vertical dimension, extra colour and an added decorative feature without any safety worries — climbers such as Ivy can be wound around each candle and flowers can clothe the base. When lit the candles provide the extra dimension of soft and flickering light, but they also provide a fire hazard if you are careless. First of all, make sure that each candle is firmly fixed in the arrangement. One way is to tape 4 cocktail sticks to the base as shown in the illustration and then push the points firmly into the foam — an easier way of securing a candle is to use a candle holder (see page 8). In either case check that the candle is not sloping. Next, make sure that there is no plant material touching the wax surface, and always snuff out the flame when the room is unoccupied

RIBBON

Bows and trailing ribbons usually belong to the world of floristry rather than the realm of flower arranger, but there are times when this accessory can add to the appeal of a display. A few hints — buy polypropylene ribbon from a florist rather than satin ribbon from the haberdashery department of a store. This plastic ribbon can be torn easily into strips and does not fray at the ends, unlike the woven variety. Next, always trim the ends with a sloping cut — curl these ends by drawing them firmly and quickly over the back of a knife. Don't try to tie a bow — the florist bow is made by folding a ribbon into a figure-of-eight as shown in the illustration, and then tying fine wire around the point held by the fingers. A double or treble figure-of-eight bow can be made by using more loops of ribbon. As with other accessories you must be careful not to overdo ribbon decoration. It is generally a welcome addition to Christmas decorations and some church displays, but it is usually out of place with ordinary living room arrangements

FIGURINE

You will either love or hate the idea of figures in wood, metal, pottery, glass etc as part of your flower arrangement. For some the presence of such an accessory provides extra interest and a way to underline the theme of the display — biblical figures next to a Christmas arrangement, a Chinese fisherman alongside an Ikebana display etc. For others such distractions are regarded as unnecessary or downright bad taste. On the show bench things are different — the 'Landscape' class so often seems to call for the use of figures of birds, small animals etc. Still, you mustn't overdo it — make sure the figurines are in scale and do not detract from the plant material. Remember that one figurine may be acceptable or even attractive, but two figurines of different sizes and materials can look ghastly when placed close together

Plant Material

This section deals with fresh flowers and foliage — dried and artificial materials are discussed in later chapters. Most arrangements are made with cut flowers and there are three basic sources for this fresh material. The prime source is the garden, where you can cut blooms which you know are absolutely fresh and at the right stage for arranging indoors. In addition there is a plentiful supply of stems and leaves which are so vital for nearly all displays, and all of this material is free. The main problem is that there are times when the supply of garden blooms is limited or when you wish to make a display which calls for bigger and brighter flowers than your garden can offer. So you have to turn to an alternative source of supply. There is the countryside — free material again, but wild flowers tend to be subtle rather than showy, and many of our more attractive native plants are protected. This means that for a supply of bold flowers to go with garden-gathered foliage and stems you must choose the third source — the flower seller. This may be a giant garden centre or a woman by the side of the road, a florist or a greengrocer, a market stall or a supermarket. Beautiful blooms perhaps, but they were picked some time ago. Choose with care and be guided by the advice on the next page.

Plant material can be divided up into three basic types. Most arrangements call for the use of all of them

LINE MATERIAL

Other name : Outline material

Line material consists of tall stems, flowering spikes or bold leaves which are used to create the basic framework or skeleton. This line material may be straight or curved, and it sets the height and width of the finished arrangement

Examples: Box, Privet, Gladiolus, long-stemmed Rose, Eucalyptus, Winter Jasmine, Broom, Forsythia, Delphinium

DOMINANT MATERIAL

Other names : Focal material, Point material

Dominant material consists of bold flowers or clusters of showy smaller blooms — eye-catching foliage is occasionally used. This dominant material provides a centre or centres of interest

Examples: Gerbera, Chrysanthemum, Anthurium, Lily, Paeony, Tulip, Poppy, Rose, Hydrangea, Dahlia, Daffodil, Geranium

FILLER MATERIAL

Other name : Secondary material

Filler material consists of smaller flowers or all sorts of leaves which are used to cover the mechanics and edges of the container, and also provide added interest and colour to the display. Unwanted bare areas are filled

Examples: Scabious, Geum, Hebe, Holly, Alstroemeria, Aster, Gypsophila, Solidago, Freesia, Ivy, Euonymus, spray Carnation

Buying Cut Flowers

WHERE TO BUY

A long-established florist obviously has a reputation to maintain, but you cannot rely on one supplier always being superior to the others. The only way to judge quality is to look at the stock — go somewhere else if the water in the flower buckets is stale and if full-price material is well past the stage described below. Most keen flower arrangers establish a relationship with a local supplier so that orders can be placed for out-of-the-ordinary flowers which are not kept in stock but are available at the wholesale market.

WHAT TO LOOK FOR

Look at the flower buckets first. They should be out of direct sunlight and the water should be clear and not smelly. The foliage should be firm and the cut ends properly immersed. As a general rule choose blooms at the **Open Stage** for a long-lasting display. At this stage multi-flowered stems have a few open blooms and plenty of coloured buds. The **Bud Stage** is too early — tight green buds do not often open indoors. The problem with the **Ripe Stage** is that all the flowers are fully open and so the display will be short-lived. Of course this is not a problem if the display is for a special occasion on the next day. With single Daisy-like blooms the Open Stage is when the petals are fully open but the central disc is free from a dusting of yellow pollen. These are general rules — see below for specific guidance.

WHEN TO BUY THE POPULAR ONES

PLANT	STAGE OF DEVELOPMENT FOR MAXIMUM VASE-LIFE
ALSTROEMERIA	A few flowers open — buds showing colour
ANEMONE	Most flowers open — centres still tight. Buds showing colour
CARNATION — SPRAY	About half flowers open — buds plump and firm
CARNATION — STANDARD	Flowers open — no white threads. Leaves firm and fresh
CHRYSANTHEMUM — SINGLE	Most flowers open. Central discs greenish — no pollen present
CHRYSANTHEMUM — DOUBLE	Flowers open — centres tight and outer petals firm
DAFFODIL — SINGLE	Buds showing colour and beginning to open
DAFFODIL — DOUBLE	Flowers fully open
FREESIA	A few flowers open — buds showing colour
GERBERA	Flowers open. Central disc greenish — no pollen present
GLADIOLUS	A few flowers open — buds showing colour
GYPSOPHILA	Nearly all flowers open
IRIS	A few flowers open — buds showing colour
LILY	A few flowers open — buds showing colour
ORCHID	Flowers fully open
RANUNCULUS	Most flowers open — centres still tight. Buds showing colour
ROSE	Open buds or tight-centred flowers. Some leaves on stems
STATICE	Nearly all flowers open
TULIP	Buds showing colour — leaves not limp

TAKING THEM HOME

Get the flowers home as quickly as possible — do not put them in the boot of a car on a warm day. Condition the blooms (see pages 16–17) before arranging them.

Gathering & Conditioning Garden Flowers

Some preparation is necessary before you can arrange the plant material which has been cut from the garden or bought from a shop. The purpose of this preparation is to ensure that there is no callus at the bottom of the stems nor any air blocks along their length. As a result water is able to flow freely up the plant material once the arrangement has been created, and this means that vase-life is extended. This process is known as **conditioning**, and for many plants there is a **pre-conditioning** stage.

STEP 1: CUTTING

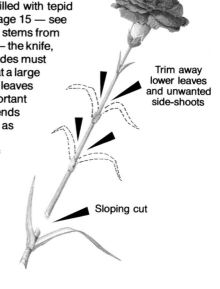

Trim away lower leaves and unwanted side-shoots

Sloping cut

Go out into the garden in the morning or evening with a bucket half-filled with tepid water. Choose flowers which are at the open stage as described on page 15 — see the table below for additional guidance. Be careful not to cut too many stems from recently-planted specimens. There are three rules concerning cutting — the knife, scissors or secateurs must be clean to avoid bacterial infection, the blades must be sharp to ensure a clean cut, and this cut must be a sloping one so that a large area of water-absorbing surface is exposed. Quickly remove the lower leaves which would be submerged in the arrangement — it is especially important that grey or downy leaves are not left in water. It is essential that the cut ends are not allowed to dry out — get the stems into the bucket as quickly as possible and keep it out of full sun.

Take the bucket indoors when cutting is finished. Read page 17 to see if Step 2 is required — if not, go on to Step 3.

CONDITIONING NON-GARDEN FLOWERS

There will be times when the plant material has not been cut from the garden and has not been in water for some time — cut flowers brought home from the florist, material gathered from the countryside, the florist bouquet delivered to the door, and so on. In this case you must re-cut the stalks under water — this sloping cut should remove about 1 in. (2.5 cm) from the stem ends. Remove the lower leaves as above, and stand the material in a partly-filled bucket. Go on to Step 3 if Step 2 is not necessary.

PLANT	STAGE OF DEVELOPMENT FOR MAXIMUM VASE-LIFE
FLORIST FLOWERS	See page 15 — same stages apply to garden-grown material
ACHILLEA	Flowers fully open
ANTIRRHINUM	Bottom half of spike in flower
CORNFLOWER	Flowers fully open
DAHLIA	Most flowers open. Central discs greenish — no pollen present
DELPHINIUM	Most of spike in flower
FORSYTHIA	Buds beginning to open
FOXGLOVE	Bottom half of spike in flower
LILAC	Most of cluster still in bud
LILY-OF-THE-VALLEY	Nearly all flowers open
LUPIN	Bottom half of spike in flower
MICHAELMAS DAISY	Nearly all flowers open
MOLUCCELLA	Flowers fully open
PELARGONIUM	Buds in cluster beginning to open
POPPY	Buds beginning to open
RHODODENDRON	Most of cluster still in bud
SCABIOUS	Buds beginning to open
SWEET PEA	A few flowers open — buds showing colour

STEP 2:
PRE-CONDITIONING if necessary

WOODY STEM TREATMENT

The bottom of woody stems (Rhododendron, Lilac, Privet, etc) require more than a sloping cut to ensure adequate exposure to water before conditioning. This calls for scraping the bark from the bottom 1–2 in. (2.5–5 cm) with a knife and then making a 1 in. (2.5 cm) slit with scissors or knife. Do not hammer the ends as this can lead to bacterial infection. Remove thorns from Roses with a knife or scissors.

MILKY SAP TREATMENT

Several flowering and foliage plants have sap which oozes out of the cut surface and then coagulates to form a waterproof seal. Singeing is the way to tackle this problem — hold a flame (cigarette lighter, match or candle) to the cut end until it is blackened. This anti-oozing technique should be applied to the milky-sap plants such as Poppy and Euphorbia as well as to Ferns, Dahlia and Zinnia.

SPRING BULB TREATMENT

Tulips, Hyacinths and Daffodils need special treatment. Cut away the white part of the stem as this zone cannot take up water efficiently — a sloping cut on the green part of the stem is needed for maximum vase-life. Some spring-flowering bulbs have sap which shortens the life of other flowers — let the stems drain by standing them in their own bucket of water overnight before conditioning.

WILTED FLOWER TREATMENT

There is no point in conditioning material which has wilted leaves and/or flowers. The answer is to use the hot-water treatment as a pick-me-up for these jaded plants — Roses and many woody plants respond dramatically to this technique. Cover blooms with a paper bag and immerse the bottom inch of the stems in near-boiling water for 1 minute. An additional benefit is the destruction of bacteria.

FLOPPY STEM TREATMENT

A number of flowering plants (e.g Tulips and Lupins) have floppy stems, and this means that they droop during the conditioning process and in the arrangement. The usual treatment is to wrap a group of stems in damp newspaper and then stand the bundle upright in water overnight. Despite treatment Tulips may quickly flop — the answer is floral wire pushed up through the stem. Prick a hole below each flower.

LARGE LEAF TREATMENT

First wash the leaves in tepid water to remove dust and surface deposits. Then immerse the leaves or leafy branches in a bowl of tepid water for several hours so that the tissues of the foliage are filled with water. Wilted flowers can sometimes be revived in this way. A few words of caution — lift out small leaves after an hour and do not use this technique for grey or downy foliage.

STEP 3:
CONDITIONING

The final step is to condition the plant material which may or may not have required a special pre-conditioning treatment. The technique is simple — the stems are immersed in tepid water in a bucket, and this container is stood in a cool and dark place for 2–8 hours. It is often helpful to add a cut flower preservative (see page 9) to the conditioning water. For most plants deep immersion is recommended. Spring-flowering bulbs are an exception — condition Tulips, Daffodils etc in shallow water. Don't leave the conditioned plants on the table when arranging — go straight from the bucket into the moist floral foam or water-filled container.

CHAPTER 3

DESIGNING YOUR ARRANGEMENT

There will have been many times in the past when you have looked at a floral display and have known that it was created by a skilled flower arranger. Of course we are impressed by sheer size and by the use of exotic blooms, but neither is essential. The arrangement which arouses instant admiration has something more — it has **harmony**. Harmony is the blending together of the seven features of good design which are listed below.

It may seem strange that a tower-like cone of flowers in a stately home can share its basic features with a delicate Oriental grouping of a twig, some foliage and a bloom or two. But expertly-arranged examples of both types of display *do* have features in common, as you will discover in this chapter.

That leaves one fundamental question which needs to be answered — must one slavishly follow all these rules about shape, colour, proportion and so on in order to be a good flower arranger? After all, most of these principles and elements are shared with other forms of artistic endeavour, yet Picasso and Rembrandt couldn't have followed the same rules!

In fact Picasso did learn the rules and styles of classical painting and he applied them at the start of his career — it was later that he evolved his own styles and techniques. Apply this principle as your approach to flower arranging — learn and practice the classical features of good floral design, and then depart from one or more if you are indeed a budding Picasso. But do this on the basis of knowing full well that you are departing from the traditional rules and principles which are well-known to you and not merely doing your own thing out of ignorance.

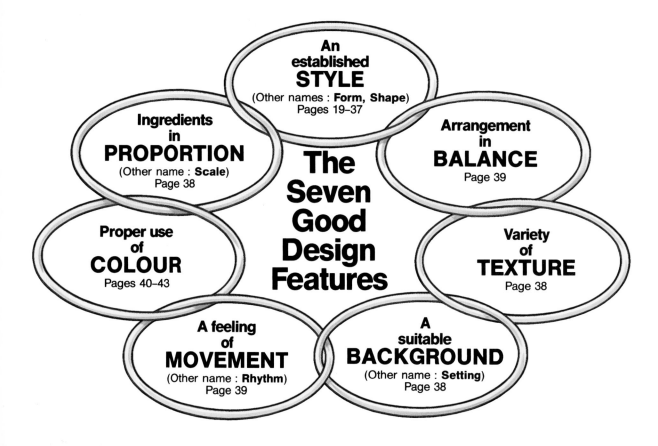

An established STYLE
(Other names : **Form, Shape**)
Pages 19–37

Ingredients in PROPORTION
(Other name : **Scale**)
Page 38

Arrangement in BALANCE
Page 39

The Seven Good Design Features

Proper use of COLOUR
Pages 40–43

Variety of TEXTURE
Page 38

A feeling of MOVEMENT
(Other name : **Rhythm**)
Page 39

A suitable BACKGROUND
(Other name : **Setting**)
Page 38

STYLES

THE ALL-ROUND ARRANGEMENT

The all-round arrangement is designed to be seen from all sides, and is therefore chosen for a table or room centrepiece display. When seen from above it is usually circular, but may be broadly oval or square

THE FACING ARRANGEMENT

The facing (or flat-back) arrangement is designed to be seen only from the front and perhaps the sides, and is therefore chosen for a shelf or sideboard display. Do not place too close to the wall

There are hundreds of different types of flower arrangements and it is not possible to fit all of them into neat pigeon-holes with clear-cut definitions. Some groupings are possible, however, to help you in your quest to find a style which will suit your skill, artistic temperament, materials available and the location where it will be placed.

First of all, you can decide between an all-round and a facing arrangement, as described on the left. Then there is the split between the informal and formal arrangement. Little pre-planning goes into the informal display — strict geometric shapes (triangles, crescents, fans etc) are avoided and instead a free-flowing natural effect is sought. With the formal display there are guidelines to follow and the placing of the plant material is planned beforehand. The shapes are generally (but not always) geometric. Surprisingly, creating a really successful informal arrangement calls for at least as much artistic talent as making an 'impressive' formal one.

All-round and facing, informal and formal — these concepts are needed in order to decide the visual effect of the finished display, but they do not help you to put a name to an arrangement you may see in a magazine or in a friend's house. Set out below is a classification adopted by some (but not all!) flower arrangers. It is based on the amount of **space** present — the proportion of air to plant material within the boundaries of the display.

Most arrangements in the Western world are made in either the Mass or Line-mass style, and for many years the formal geometric shape has been dominant. But things are changing — the trend is towards simpler, less stylised displays which have an irregular shape.

The MASS Style
Little or no open space is enclosed within the boundary of the arrangement — any space present is not a basic requirement of the style

The LINE Style
Open space within the boundary of the arrangement is a key feature — much or all of the display is line material as described on page 14

The LINE-MASS Style
Some open space is present within the boundary of the arrangement — only part of the area between the framework of line material is filled with leaves and/or flowers

The MISCELLANEOUS Style
An arrangement which does not belong to any of the above styles, or an arrangement which can be made in two or all three of these styles

The MASS Style

Little or no open space is enclosed within the boundary of the arrangement — any space present is not a basic requirement of the style. The Mass style originated in Europe, beginning according to tradition with the Renaissance and first glorified in the paintings of the Dutch Masters in the 17th century. The style came into full flower with the table and room arrangements of the late Victorian era — silver trumpets packed with flowers and foliage, roughly oval in outline and often a kaleidoscope of colour. The 20th century has been a period of modification — the triangle has become the most popular shape and arrangements have become much looser and less formal.

The Mass style has several basic features. Generally the arrangement is an all-round one, and line material is used to create a skeleton of an upright axis and several horizontal laterals. This framework is then more or less completely covered with flowers and/or other plant material. There is usually no attempt to make any particular part a distinct focal point and transition is considered important. Transition means that changes within the arrangement are gradual rather than abrupt — colours, shapes etc of neighbouring blooms tend to blend together rather than stand out in sharp contrast. In the 1980s the Natural approach became popular — plant material is massed together "like flowers in the garden, with enough space for the butterflies."

The MASS Style

BUNCH IN A VASE

◁ This is the simplest arrangement, and also the *only* one for millions of people. The stem bases of a shop-bought or florist-delivered bunch are cut and then the flowers put in a vase which is half-filled with water. In summer a variety of blooms are taken from the garden and treated in a similar way. All too often the effect is stiff and the display is short-lived, so a few hints may be useful. Condition the flowers before you start (see pages 16–17) and most floral arrangements can be improved by adding some foliage from the garden. Cut the stems to different lengths to give the display a roughly triangular shape. For a more natural and free-flowing effect make a **tied bunch** — see page 45 for details.

BIEDERMEIER

This arrangement is a flat or domed mass floral display in a round and ▷ shallow container — the flowers may be fresh, dried or artificial. In the true Biedermeier the blooms are arranged to give concentric circles of different colours and there is an outer collar of foliage. The term, however, is used nowadays for any circular low arrangement where the stems are almost completely hidden. The Biedermeier has long been used as a table arrangement and continues to be popular. A single flower type or a medley of different blooms can be used — a good way to display spring flowers or Roses. Other names include **posy** and **domed display** — mechanics may or may not be used.

TRADITIONAL MASS

◁ Traditional is the usual term for the classic massed arrangement which is held in place by floral foam or crumpled chicken wire. The use of these mechanics allows displays of various shapes to be created — oval, fan etc. The most popular outline these days is the triangle, but this shape was surprisingly rare before World War II. The Traditional arrangement is to be seen everywhere in sizes ranging from table centrepieces to ceiling-high displays. In all cases the first step should be to create a central upright axis with line material and then the dominant flowers should be inserted. The final step is to use filler material to cover all or nearly all of the line material.

BYZANTINE CONE

This ancient-style arrangement is not recommended for the display of ▷ fresh flowers — it is difficult to keep moist, the effect is extremely formal and a lot of plant material is required. The mechanic is traditionally a moss-filled wire frame but these days a floral foam cone is used. A modern Byzantine cone is worth considering for a few special situations. Dried or artificial flowers are used — the surface of the brown floral foam is first covered with leafy sprigs and then a variety of short-stemmed blooms, fruits, berries, accessories etc are added to provide interest and colour. A large display in a grand and formal setting can be impressive, and in the home it can provide an attractive addition to Christmas decorations.

The MASS Style

A Bunch in a Vase. Blooms are usually placed haphazardly in this style of arrangement to give a natural feel, but not in this display. The Lilies and Gazanias have been grouped in distinct blocks — a modern approach to an age-old style. ▷

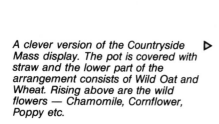

◁ The Round version of the Traditional Mass style. The mechanics of floral foam and chicken wire are the centre point of the circle, and strong line material is used to form the spokes of the wheel. A tall pot or pedestal is required.

A clever version of the Countryside Mass display. The pot is covered with straw and the lower part of the arrangement consists of Wild Oat and Wheat. Rising above are the wild flowers — Chamomile, Cornflower, Poppy etc. ▷

The MASS Style

◁ *The classical type of Biedermeier — concentric rings of flowers above a collar of leaves — red Roses, white Saxifrage and blue Grape Hyacinths. The modern Biedermeier is a much simpler and less formal affair — a domed display of randomly-placed blooms in a shallow container.*

A Traditional Mass display which seems to have stepped out of an old Dutch painting. It appears to have been thrown together, but a good deal of skill is required to create the vibrance associated with this type of arrangement. ▷

◁ *The Bulb version of the Bunch in a Vase. Soft-stemmed spring bulbs such as Tulips and Bluebells from the garden are often placed in tall water-filled vases so that little of the stem is exposed. The heads droop after a day or two, but the display is not spoiled.*

The LINE Style

Open space within the boundary of the arrangement is a key feature — much or all of the display is line material as described on page 14. The Line style is the opposite of the Mass design in nearly every way. Origin, mechanics and the choice and use of plant material are all quite different. The Line concept originated in the East and rules were laid down in China more than 1000 years ago — the Mass style is a product of the West and began much later. The basic feature of a Line design is limited use of plant material with support often provided by a pinholder — in the traditional Mass arrangement there are lots of flowers and/or foliage supported in either floral foam or crumpled chicken wire.

These are perhaps details — the fundamental feature of the Line style is that each element of the design is important in its own right and the air space contained within the framing line material is vital to the overall effect of the display. As the name indicates, it is the *lines* and not the *mass* which are the main source of appeal. Another key difference is that transition (page 20) is not important — in fact it is positively undesirable with many Line arrangements. We do not know just when the Line style was adopted in the West — Ikebana aroused much interest when exhibited at the first Chelsea Flower Show in 1912, but it was in the U.S between 1955 and 1975 that the Western Line style really took hold.

The LINE Style

VERTICAL

◁ The Vertical arrangement is the only type of Line style which is formal, geometric and defined by clear-cut rules. The all-important feature is bold line material which is set vertically to form a central axis. This may be a single leafy stem, a small group of narrow leaves or tall flowering stems of Rose, Liatris etc. At the base are short wings of foliage to cover the mechanics — variegated Hosta, feathery Fern or leathery Rhododendron are typical examples. The third plant element is the single or small group of dominant flowers placed along the axis or close to the base of the arrangement — Anthurium, Gerbera, Lily etc. Note the absence of filler plant material.

IKEBANA

Ikebana or Japanese-style flower arranging has been practised for ▷ many hundreds of years, but it remains a mystery to the Western mind. The 'two sticks and a flower' slur shows how little we understand the wealth of symbolism behind the deceptively simple arrangements — Ikebana ('making flowers live') is a path to self-enlightenment and not just a way of doing the flowers for millions of Japanese. It is not possible, of course, to describe even the fundamental principles in a few words, but you can create a simple design by following the magical rule of three. Arrange three pieces of line material with three different heights or centres of interest — highest is Heaven, Man is central and Earth is lowest. See page 26 for more details.

FREE-STYLE

◁ During the 1960s a new style appeared — asymmetrical, irregular in outline and sparse. The important feature is that the line material is left mainly uncovered by flowers and/or foliage, and any additional plant material is generally bold and eye-catching. Contrasting colours are now no longer feared and there is little or no attempt to cover spaces within the design with filler material. The container is generally fully exposed, which means that it must be chosen with care as it will be part of the design. No tedious rules, a display to fit in with today's life-style, but there is no agreement over the name for this Western Line arrangement — **Modern**, **Contemporary** and **Free-line** have all been used.

ABSTRACT

In the progression from the formal and traditional Mass style to the ▷ informal and irregular Line designs of today, the Abstract arrangement is the final stop. It takes Free-style a stage further. This is no longer a flower arrangement as such — it is a piece of three-dimensional modern art in which living and/or dead plant material is used as the decorative medium. It is an art form, and the plant material may be painted or sliced. The definition may seem straightforward, but in practice there is no clear-cut line between the Free-style and Abstract designs. This style has been around for many years, but it was not until the 1980s that the public started to take notice.

The LINE Style

The Nageire style dates originally from the ▷
12th century. It is a classical arrangement
in a tall cylindrical vase — the effect is
flowing and natural. In this slanting version
the long horizontal stem is the Heaven line.

◁ *The Shoka (Seika) style began in the 18th*
century. It is a formal arrangement with
strict rules governing the lengths and
angles of the stems. It is basically a
triangular and usually stiff style in which
all the stems arise from a single point.

The Moribana style was created at the ▷
beginning of this century. It is an
informal arrangement in a shallow
container in which a pinholder is
placed. Landscapes are portrayed or
large, colourful flowers are displayed.

◁ *The ultimate simplicity in Line arrangement — a bunch of twigs in a bowl. Not for everyone, of course, but this style can look stunning with dramatic lighting in a stark, modern interior. An arrangement for the artist, as material selection and placing call for much skill.*

A piece of Modern Art created with plant ▷ material. The central core of the Pitcher Plants (Sarracenia) in this Free-style arrangement is surrounded by narrow-headed grass stems above and a large daisy-head below.

◁ *The eye-catching intricate pattern of skeletonised Ponga bark from New Zealand is contrasted with the solidity of the oranges in this Abstract design by Marian Aaronson. The large dried leaves create further areas of interest.*

The **LINE-MASS** Style

Some open space is present within the boundary of the arrangement — only part of the area between the framework of line material is filled with leaves and/or flowers. The period between 1950 and 1965 was an exciting time for flower arranging. The pioneering work by people like Constance Spry and Julia Clements continued to popularise the idea that making a flower arrangement could be an artistically-satisfying experience and not just a way of bringing garden flowers indoors. Equally important was the appearance of floral foam which made possible for everyone the creation of impressive displays. In light of this rapidly-growing interest in arranging flowers, the marriage of the Western Mass style and the Line style from the East was inevitable.

Line-mass became an important concept — a style in which the skeleton formed by line material was clothed but not covered by other flowers and/or foliage. The early teachers set out guidelines but unfortunately these were regarded as rules, and so for many years geometric patterns were carefully reproduced. Dominant material was dutifully grouped at the base and filler material was used to ensure a neat transition between the various elements. Things have now loosened up — irregular designs are now popular. This style is excellent for natural arrangements ... after all, the garden with its twiggy shrubs above the massed flowers in the border is really a Line-mass arrangement!

The LINE-MASS Style

SYMMETRICAL TRIANGLE

◁ For forty years the Symmetrical triangle has remained the most popular Line-mass arrangement. In the beginning strict formality was the rule, with the two horizontal ribs at the base being composed of the same line materials and the two sides of the triangle being almost identical to each other. This somewhat stiff arrangement is sometimes sneeringly referred to as the 'florist' design but it must be remembered that it persists because of its popular appeal. There is a feeling of solidity and perfect balance, but these days a looser and less formal approach is generally preferred. A wider variety of line material is used and the outline is flowing and uneven.

ASYMMETRICAL TRIANGLE

The Asymmetrical triangle is even less formal and often more eye- ▷ catching than the modern version of its more popular symmetrical sister. The lateral ribs are markedly different in length so that the arrangement has a distinctly off-centred or L-shaped look and the basal flowers and/or leaves often drape gracefully over the edge of the container. With a bold centre of interest and an interesting range of filler material this design is a good choice for the show bench. It also fits in well with modern decor, but in more traditional surroundings a pair of arrangements which are mirror images of each other are sometimes placed side by side to create a more balanced feel.

CRESCENT

◁ An attractive arrangement for a foam-filled shallow dish — not much material is required but it must be chosen with care. The usual approach is to use bare, leafy or flowering woody stems from the garden to create the curved outline and then to add either home-grown or shop-bought flowers and foliage at the centre. You may be fortunate enough to find suitably arched woody shoots, but it is usually necessary to bend them after cutting — see Hogarth curve below. These curved stems are pushed into the ends of the block with one side appreciably higher than the other — the secret of success is to create the impression that the crescent is made from a group of uncut stems. Hide the mechanics with dominant and filler material.

HOGARTH CURVE

The elongated S was the 'line of beauty' described by the painter ▷ William Hogarth. The Hogarth curve design is based on this shape and it is showy and full of movement. But it is also highly formal, and its popularity has declined with the trend away from geometric arrangements. In order to create the S outline you will need two sets of matched curved stems for placing in the foam block at the top of a tall container. Long and pliable shoots are used — examples include Broom, Flowering Currant, Winter Jasmine and Rosemary. Soak the stems in water, tie the ends together with string to create a curved shape and leave to dry for several hours. Hide the mechanics with dominant and filler material.

The **LINE-MASS** Style

INVERTED CRESCENT

A popular arrangement for the centre of the dining room table where ▷
candles are to be included — a candle cup (see page 11) together with
a candle holder are used. The display will have to be an all-round one
(page 19) with the line material at the base forming a circle or an oval,
depending on the shape of the table. The Inverted crescent may also
be used as a facing display in a tall container such as a tazza (page 11)
or in a vase or urn on a pedestal. Here the vertical line material is short-
stemmed and the horizontal line material is naturally pendent. This
drooping effect is heightened by using lengths of soft-stemmed filler
material such as Ivy and Alchemilla around the base.

HORIZONTAL

◁ A popular arrangement for the centre of the dining room table where
candles are not to be included and an unobstructed view of people
around the table is required. A low rectangular container is generally
used and either fresh or dried material can be employed. The basic
difference compared with the Inverted crescent is that the basal line
material is stiff rather than drooping. Many plants are suitable —
Gladiolus, long-stemmed Rose, Box, spray Carnation etc depending
on the size of the arrangement. Of course the design is not truly
horizontal — at some point a short vertical axis is placed which is
usually a centre of interest (focal point) but need not be in the middle of
the display.

FAN

In some ways the Fan is the opposite of the Horizontal display — the ▷
upright ribs or axes are spreading and showy, and the arrangement is
at its best when it is large. Use the Fan to cover the fireplace in summer
or in the hall as a prominent display on a pedestal. Five, seven or nine
stems of line material are set like spokes in the mechanics. Flowering
material is often used — examples include Liatris, Lily, Gladiolus, long-
stemmed Rose and Iris. This framework should then be partly filled in
with dominant and filler material. Dried flowers make excellent Fan
arrangements — suitable line materials for the spokes include Wheat,
Reed Mace, Chinese Lantern, Banksia and long-stemmed Rose.

INFORMAL

◁ It is easy to understand the basic principles of an Informal arrangement. It is a Line-mass style with the ribs formed from line material
which is partly but not entirely covered by dominant and filler material,
and with an overall outline which is irregular. The artistic ability of the
arranger is given free rein as there is no need to create a geometric
pattern, and both the symmetry and placing of centres of interest are
completely up to you. A few words of warning — the tight rules
concerning shape are abandoned but forgetting the principles of
colour, proportion, background and movement can result in a mess.
Secondly, it is easier to create a pleasing formal rather than an informal
arrangement if you are not artistic.

The **LINE-MASS** Style

◁ *The Inverted Crescent was very popular before the introduction of modern styles such as Parallel, Free-style etc. Its geometric nature is considered old-fashioned by some, but here it has been given an up-to-date treatment with colours in distinct blocks.*

This type of Rose arrangement can be seen ▷ *in homes throughout the country in summer, but it is not easy to classify. The tall blooms form the distinct and partially uncovered ribs associated with Line-mass, but it is Rose foliage and not added plants which provide the filler material.*

◁ *A good example of Informal Line-mass which fits in so well with modern decor. Montbretia, Gladioli, Red Hot Poker and Willow twigs are the line material — a vertical series of Achillea flower-heads make up the dominant material.*

The **MISCELLANEOUS** Style

An arrangement which does not belong to any of the basic styles (Mass, Line or Line-mass), or an arrangement which can be made in two or all three of these styles. The Miscellaneous group is a hotch-potch of arrangements which do not fit neatly into any of the types described on the previous pages. Firstly, there are the Miscellaneous styles which are defined by their size rather than the way the plant material is used — the diminutive Miniatures and Petites at one extreme and the impressive Grand displays at the other. With the second set of Miscellaneous arrangements the key feature is that the plant material does not appear to radiate from a single point — the Landscape and Parallel styles belong here. The third set are massed arrangements in unusual forms — the round Wreaths, the elongated Swags and Garlands, and the Topiary tree with its 'trunk' and not the floral material set in the container. Finally, there is the Pot-et-fleur arrangement which brings cut flowers and house plants together.

The make-up of this Miscellaneous group can be expected to change over the years. Some designs will move out and others will be added. The Parallel style may well become popular enough to give rise to several variations and so become a major style group on its own, whereas quite new ways of using plant material may be conceived and give rise to arrangements which find a home in this Miscellaneous group of styles.

The **MISCELLANEOUS** Style

PARALLEL

◁ During the 1980s a revolutionary new style spread from Holland — the Parallel or **European** style. In these arrangements the mechanic is generally a rectangular block of floral foam set in a shallow dish, and from it arises the key feature — groups of stems which stand vertically. This line material is not covered up by other plants, although the foam is hidden by a horizontal groundwork of flowers, foliage, fruits, stems etc. There is no transition (see page 20) — blocks of contrasting shapes and colours are placed next to each other, and the vertical lines emerge directly from the horizontal mass. The overall design may be Line or Line-mass, depending on the amount of plant material used, and often (but not always) a 'natural' look is aimed for.

LANDSCAPE

The Landscape arrangement is more at home on the show bench than ▷ in the living room or hall — it is an interpretive style. The goal is to create a representation of a tiny piece of the environment — a meadow, wood, beach etc. The result can look a mess unless a few well-established rules are followed. Use a container and base which are in keeping with the theme and do not overdo it — use restrained hints to picture the scene rather than to make a fully-clothed miniature garden. A well-shaped branch can indicate a tree, a few pebbles for the shore, and so on. Next, scale is important — make sure the flowers around your 'tree' are small. Finally, limit the size and numbers of accessories — they should not dominate the scene.

MINIATURE and PETITE

◁ The small-scale flower arrangement calls for not much material but a good deal of skill. The problem is that a small error which may not be noticed in a standard-sized arrangement can appear to be a glaring error when the whole thing is only a few inches high. In Britain (but not all countries) the size of a Miniature arrangement is a maximum of 4 in. (10 cm) high, wide and deep — a Petite should not exceed 9 in. (23 cm) high, wide and deep. There is, of course, some latitude when it is for the home, but in show work it is vital to stay within these limits. Keeping things in scale is the main challenge — container, plant material and accessories must all be in proportion. You can use fresh or preserved material — dried arrangements make excellent gifts.

GRAND

These displays are at the other end of the scale to the Miniature and ▷ Petite — the Grand display stands at least 3 ft (1 metre) high and is to be seen in churches, stately homes, hotel foyers and other public buildings. The basic style is Mass or Line-mass, but a Line arrangement can be an excellent choice for ultra-modern surroundings. It may be all-round or facing, and florist cones (page 7) are used to enable relatively short-stemmed blooms to be included. The most usual arrangement is the **Pedestal** display — a triangular Mass style studded with bold and filler flowers covering the line material. Trailing plants are used to soften or hide the edge of the container. Chicken wire rather than floral foam is the usual mechanic and a large container is essential.

The MISCELLANEOUS Style

WREATH

In Britain Wreaths are usually associated with either funerals or ▷
Christmas, but these circular arrangements are excellent for both table
and wall display. There are various types of mechanics or containers as
described on page 11 — the best, perhaps, are green floral foam for
fresh plant material and brown foam or a woven cane ring for a dried or
artificial display. The first stage is to cover the foam or cane with short
lengths of leafy sprigs and then add flowers, fruits, seed-heads etc. The
final step is to attach accessories (ribbons, baubles etc) if required. At
Christmas, wreath frames covered with natural or artificial leafy
material are available for covering with flowers, ribbons and seasonal
ornaments.

GARLAND and SWAG

◁ A Garland is an elongated massed flower arrangement which is
flexible and is designed for winding around pillars, banisters etc. A
Swag on the other hand is for hanging rather than twining — either as a
vertical display by suspending it from the top or as a drooping curve by
suspending it from either side. There are several ways to construct
Garlands and Swags by using moss-filled chicken wire tubes, lengths
of rope etc, and ready-made foam-filled plastic mesh tubes are
available. The easiest way to make your own is to buy a number of floral
foam blocks which are first covered with and then twisted in thin
polyethylene sheet like a string of sausages. Cover with plant material.

TOPIARY TREE

Garlands and Wreaths have been made and used for adornment for ▷
thousands of years, but the Topiary tree is a product of this century. It
can be made with fresh flowers, but it means a lot of material and
trouble for a short display life — the Topiary tree should be regarded as
a dried or artificial flower arrangement. Choose a trunk — a natural
bark-covered branch is better than a broom-handle. Set one end in
cement or plaster of paris in a suitable pot — insert the other end in a
floral foam ball once the trunk is set in the container. Insert sprigs of
foliage material until the mechanics are hidden and then stud the
surface with flowers, berries, cones, fruits etc.

POT-ET-FLEUR

◁ The Pot-et-fleur display was first described by Violet Stevenson in
1960. It is essentially a container in which a group of house plants are
grown. During its construction a florist cone (see page 7) is sunk into
the peat between the plants. Subsequently the tube is partly filled with
water and then used to house a group of cut flowers. The idea has
never become popular, despite the obvious advantages. House plants
are much happier when grouped together, and the foliage display can
be brightened by flowers which can be easily replaced as the seasons
change. The reason for this lack of popularity is that flower arrangers
find the Pot-et-fleur too limiting for their skills. It is not really a flower
arrangement — it is a house plant display brightened up by floral
material.

◁ *A Plaque is a flower arrangement which is attached to a flat background — the display is designed for hanging on or against a vertical surface. Dried plant material is the usual medium, but here fresh white Lilies and Carnations have been used with dried material for a church display.*

A floor-to-ceiling version of the Grand arrangement. Such large-scale displays can be seen at National shows, church festivals, grand hotels and stately homes, but have no place in ordinary home flower arranging. ▷

◁ *A Parallel arrangement of garden flowers and house plants. This is the Open version with the upright line material widely spaced above the 'meadow' of groundwork plants. In the Closed version the vertical stems are much closer together and give a near-Mass effect.*

The **MISCELLANEOUS** Style

You will have to use dried flowers if you ▷
want a long-lasting Wreath — such
arrangements are very popular at
Christmas time. Fresh Wreaths do have
a place for the one-day special
occasion — on the door as in the
illustration or on the dining room table.

◁ The Swag like the Wreath is usually made with
dried or artificial plant material. The problem is
keeping fresh flowers alive, as it is difficult to
water the floral foam or moss used to support
the plants. Still, as with the Church Festival, the
fresh Swag can provide an attractive short-lived
display.

This formalised spring Landscape ▷
arrangement has been made in the
traditional style for such displays. A piece
of Contorted Willow provides the tree and
a variety of spring flowers form the
meadow — Daffodils, Grape Hyacinth,
Viburnum, Polyanthus, Pussy Willow etc.
No accessories have been used.

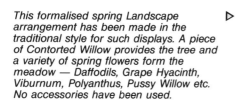

The **MISCELLANEOUS** Style

◁ *The Garland is one of the most ancient of all arrangements and is still popular for decorating pillars and posts for special occasions. Dried and artificial material is generally used but a fresh Garland has a special charm. In this one at Chester Cathedral China Aster, Ivy and Selaginella were used.*

This Petite arrangement of garden flowers (Toadflax, Candytuft, Violets, etc) is housed in a shell — a favourite container for Petite and Miniature arrangements. The display on page 33 is a Miniature — it is surprisingly difficult to make a reasonably successful one. ▷

◁ *Topiary trees tend to be small displays of dried material like the example on page 34 — moss-covered mechanics studded with flat-faced flowers. A tall tree with fresh material is an unusual but eye-catching display. This one was made with fruit, vegetables and garden flowers — note the flower group at the base.*

PROPORTION

Classic good proportion 'Golden Ratio'

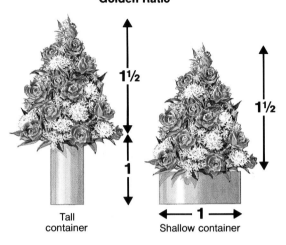

Tall container

Shallow container

A flower arrangement is made up of several elements which may be visible — container, plant material and possibly a base and accessories. Good proportion means the size of each of these elements should result in a pleasing appearance for the arrangement as a whole — very simply, everything should be in scale. The judge at the flower show will consider 'proportion' and 'scale' as two different design features, but the difference is too small and subtle for you to worry about. As stated on page 33 it is with the Landscape, Petite and Miniature arrangements that poor proportion is most likely to be seen, with oversized flowers and accessories as the main culprits. But out-of-scale arrangements can occur with any style, and the most common fault is to have a container which is the wrong size for the plant material. For centuries the Golden Ratio illustrated on the left has been used as the yardstick for perfect proportion. It will certainly satisfy the show judges and look 'right' in the home, but it is often ignored where a Line or other dramatic arrangement is created.

BACKGROUND

The arrangement may be perfectly in proportion but it can be quite wrong for the background or setting in which it has been placed. To avoid a problem there are several aspects to consider. First of all there is the style of the room — obviously an Abstract arrangement would look out of place in a chintzy cottage setting. The size of the room is equally important — a Petite arrangement in a large and lofty hall can look pathetic. The type of wall surface is important — an ornately-patterned wallpaper makes a poor backcloth for a facing arrangement placed against it, and so does a white or cream wall for an arrangement filled with pale-coloured flowers. There are also practical problems to avoid — dining table arrangements which obstruct conversation and hall arrangements which obstruct free passage are examples. 'Background' has a different meaning at the flower show — it is the structure behind the flower arrangement. You have to decorate this background so that the overall effect of the display is enhanced.

TEXTURE

Plant material comes in all sorts of textures — glossy, velvety, downy, dull, prickly etc. A glossy flower is brightened when placed next to matt foliage, and shiny leaves in strong lighting make the arrangement sparkle. A variety of textures within the arrangement increases interest by avoiding monotony, but this is perhaps the least important of the good design features of the Mass and Line-mass styles.

BALANCE

Symmetrical Arrangement

Right side equal in weight to left-hand side

Physical balance is vital — if the arrangement is markedly asymmetrical then there is a danger that the whole display will tip over. For this reason the mechanics must always be securely fixed and the container should always be heavy enough to support the plant material. The more one-sided the display, the heavier the container should be — add sand, gravel etc if necessary. **Visual balance** is not the same thing — this calls for the arrangement to *look* stable even if it is clearly one-sided. There are various ways to increase the visual weight of the lighter side — dark flowers look heavier than pale ones, and round flowers look heavier than trumpet-shaped ones. So far we have been talking about side-to-side balance — but there is also top-to-bottom balance. Large flowers placed centrally and close to the bottom of the arrangement give a feeling of good balance — incorrect placement can make the display look unbalanced, as shown below.

Asymmetrical Arrangement

Right side not equal in weight to left-hand side

Top heavy

Bottom heavy

MOVEMENT

Movement involves using techniques and materials which move the eye from one part of the display to another — this movement is due to **rhythm** being present in the design. Without rhythm (for example, a bunch of Roses in full flower stuck in a vase) the arrangement looks static and monotonous. There are various ways of producing movement and six of them are illustrated on this page.

With most all-round traditional arrangements that is the end of the story, but with many facing Line-mass displays and with most Free-style arrangements another design principle is incorporated — **dominance**. This involves having one or more areas in the arrangement to which the eye is drawn and rests there for a short time — this area is known as a **focal point** or **centre of interest**. The usual method is to include a small group of bold flowers — described in this book as dominant material. There are other ways of creating focal points — an unusual container, striking foliage, a beautiful background to a show exhibit and so on. The golden rule is that you must never overdo it — no item should be so dominant as to detract the eye for long from the rest of the display. For this reason a single large flower, especially if it is white or a bright hue, should be generally avoided as a focal point in a standard Line-mass arrangement.

Use some curved stems

Hide all or part of tall, straight stems

Have an irregular line of various-sized blooms

Use foliage of various sizes and contrasting shapes

Have flowers at various stages of development

Place flowers 'in' and 'out' in the arrangement

COLOUR

Colour is one of the first things you notice when looking at an arrangement, and so some understanding of colour is useful. This does not mean that you have to learn and then slavishly follow a lot of rules. Some of the so-called rules are suspect and far too much has been written about what goes with what and how to avoid colour clashes — "never put pink next to dark crimson" and so on. Colour is a matter of personal taste.

However, if the arrangement is for exhibition then you will have to learn and apply the rules of Colour Theory set out by the National Society (NAFAS in Britain) and which will be in the judges' manual. The basis of this theory is the colour wheel which is shown on page 41 — you will see that it is made up of numerous pure hues from which shades and tints are derived. There are basically three ways of putting these colours together in a harmonious way — that is, in a way so that the viewer will feel that they 'go together'. The boldest way is to use contrasting colours which face each other across the wheel, the most restful way is to use analogous colours which are situated next to each other and the most subtle way is to use the tints and shades of a single hue.

If you are arranging flowers for home display rather than for the flower show then you can ignore the colour wheel and its associated schemes if you like — the arrangement will be judged solely by its visual appeal and not by whether you have followed classic colour theory. In this case you should try to get a clear understanding of the properties of warm and cool colours (see page 41) and to ensure that the colours chosen are right for the room, the lighting, the season, the container and the design needs of the arrangement.

Choosing a Colour Scheme

WHAT IS THE ROOM LIKE ?

 Look at the colour of the walls, furnishings etc — try to pick up one of the important ones in the plant material you choose. Remember the importance of the background as noted on page 38. A dark-coloured display will stand out well against a pale wall but will be dimmed by a dark oak panel or maroon curtains. On the other hand a pale or warm-coloured arrangement is enhanced by a dark background — see the illustrations on pages 29 and 30 as examples.

HOW IS THE ROOM LIT ?

 Beware the dark corner. Blue or violet flowers may glisten in sunlight, but in a dimly-lit site may well disappear from view — use pale colours in shady spots. At night the colours are affected by the source of artificial lighting:

TUNGSTEN BULB		*The cool colours are dulled* *The warm colours are brightened*
FLUORESCENT TUBE		*The cool colours are brightened* *The warm colours are dulled*
CANDLELIGHT		*The cool colours are blackened* *The warm colours are yellowed*

WHAT IS THE SEASON OF THE YEAR ?

 In Japan the season is all-important in deciding the choice of plant material colour — in the Western world it is an important consideration. Spring is a time for yellows and blues, summer for a polychromatic medley (page 43), autumn calls for browns with oranges and yellows, and Christmas is the time for white and bright red.

WHAT CONTAINER WILL BE USED ?

 A common mistake is to have a container which is colourful enough to detract from the arrangement. If you do plan to use a bright or strongly-patterned vase or bowl then you should pick up the colour in the arrangement, or else the container will become an over-prominent focal point. Surprisingly this applies to white — always use some white flowers in an arrangement made in such a container.

HOW CAN THE COLOURS ENHANCE THE ARRANGEMENT ?

 Do not use equal amounts of different colours in your scheme — let one dominate and be enriched by the others. Do not spread the various colours evenly over the display or you will end up with a 'spotted dog' effect — group some of the colours together. Give your arrangement depth by having dark-coloured flowers deep in the display ('in') and lighter ones on the surface ('out'). Be careful with hues — they tend to be dominant. The classic recommendation is to use hues in small amounts and to rely mainly on tints and shades. Tints are easy to fit in to most schemes as they combine well with each other, but shades tend to be dull.

The Colour Wheel

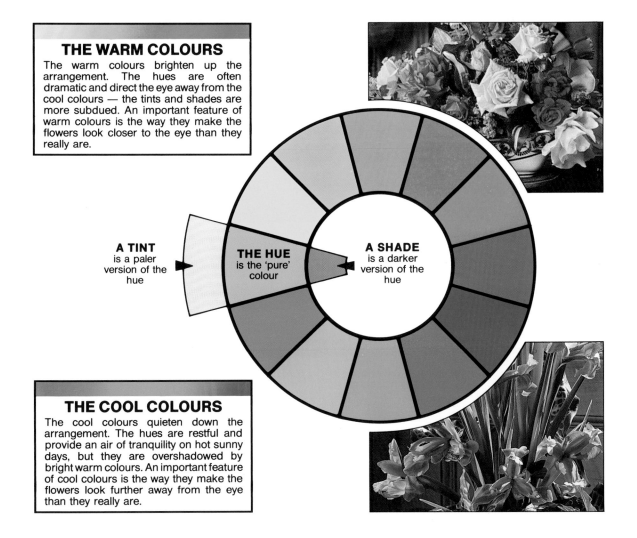

THE WARM COLOURS
The warm colours brighten up the arrangement. The hues are often dramatic and direct the eye away from the cool colours — the tints and shades are more subdued. An important feature of warm colours is the way they make the flowers look closer to the eye than they really are.

A TINT is a paler version of the hue

THE HUE is the 'pure' colour

A SHADE is a darker version of the hue

THE COOL COLOURS
The cool colours quieten down the arrangement. The hues are restful and provide an air of tranquility on hot sunny days, but they are overshadowed by bright warm colours. An important feature of cool colours is the way they make the flowers look further away from the eye than they really are.

Colour Schemes

MONOCHROMATIC

In a monochromatic scheme the various tints and shades of a single hue are used.

This is the easiest way to ensure that you will capture the mood you are trying to create — choose red for a dramatic effect, yellow for brightness, blue for a restful effect and so on. Do use a wide range of the basic colour if you can, varying from pale tints to the darkest shades. Stems and/or leaves are available in tints and shades of green, brown or white, so a 'true' monochromatic scheme is only available in these colours. An important point to remember is that the limited variation of colour means that the physical form of the display is more noticeable — aim for an assortment of shapes, sizes, textures etc.

ANALOGOUS

In an analogous (or adjacent) scheme the two, three or four hues are all neighbours on the wheel.

Such an arrangement has some of the subdued charm of the monochromatic scheme but there is a much larger range of plants from which to make your choice. There is no need to keep to the hues — tints and shades are very important here and will add to the interest of the display. An analogous scheme can be muted and restrained by working with just blues and mauves or it can be exciting with reds and purples. The addition of white filler material will add brightness to a pastel display. Do not use each colour in equal amounts — let one dominate. In the illustrated example the yellow hues and shades are dominated by the oranges and browns.

CONTRASTING

In a contrasting (or complementary) scheme the chosen colours are directly across from each other on the wheel.

With a modern Line arrangement the aim is often to create maximum impact with flower colour and so hues are used — blue Iris with orange Gerbera, yellow Rose with violet Lisianthus and so on. Contrasting schemes are always lively but they need not be over-bright. The secret is to use tints of the colours involved to produce a pastel arrangement — pink with powder blues, buffs alongside lilac-coloured blooms etc. In this way a contrasting scheme can be as subdued as an analogous one. Another approach is to use the tint of one colour and a shade of the contrasting one.

POLYCHROMATIC

In a polychromatic (or rainbow) scheme colours from all or scattered parts of the wheel are used.

In summertime flowers are sometimes collected from all over the garden and then arranged to give a display which is a multicoloured mixture spanning the spectrum. Reds and violets, yellows and blues, oranges and purples — the result can be pleasing but all too often it is not. First of all, the effect may be just too bright, and it is usually wise to look for tints of the various hues. Next, the effect may be too spotty — avoid using all the colours in equal amounts. Let just a few colours dominate the display and use the others as restrained filler material to add extra interest and transition.

CHAPTER 4

MAKING YOUR ARRANGEMENT

You are now ready to start. In previous chapters you have read about the various ingredients which go to make up an arrangement — the plant material, container, mechanics etc. You will also have learnt about the principles of good design — the various styles and the importance of proportion, balance, movement and so on.

It is now time to make an arrangement. The method will depend on three basic factors — the style you have chosen to follow, the amount and type of plant material you have assembled and the mechanics you have decided to use. This means that the amount and sort of work you have to do varies quite widely from one arrangement to another, but there are a few principles which apply generally — the Ten Golden Rules.

THE TEN GOLDEN RULES

● Keep all your flower arranging bits and pieces together rather than scattering them around the house in various drawers and cupboards. The best plan is to have one or more boxes containing mechanics and equipment in a cupboard which stores a range of containers.

● Before you begin lay a piece of waterproof sheeting over the work surface and have all the things you will need around you.

● Decide on the style of the arrangement and have a rough idea of its size before choosing the container and plant material.

● Choose the container with care — make sure it is waterproof if you are using fresh flowers. The commonest mistake is to choose a vase, dish or bowl which is either too big or too bright for the arrangement.

● Choose the plants with care. You will need line and dominant material — see page 14. For a Mass or Line-mass arrangement you will also need some filler material. See page 15 for general guidance and Chapter 11 for specific information on when to buy or cut — in nearly all cases the flowers are past their best if they are all fully open and yellow pollen is present.

● The general rule is to put in the line material first to form the basic skeleton, and then to place the dominant plant material with care. Filler material is added last of all to provide transition, extra interest and a cover for the mechanics.

● With Triangular and Fan arrangements the stems should be inserted so that they appear to arise from a point within the mechanics. With Crescent arrangements the line material should appear to pass through the mechanics.

● Avoid dullness and monotony. Stems should be different lengths, dark flowers should be set deeper in the arrangement than pale-coloured ones and not all the flowers should face directly forward.

● Stand back occasionally to check on progress — remember that the viewer will see the finished work when more than an arm's length away.

● Clean thoroughly and dry all equipment when you have finished. Remember that good aftercare of the arrangement is necessary for satisfactory vase-life — see page 51.

Mechanics: NONE

Example:
Mass Style — Tied Bunch in a Vase

STEP 1:
CHOOSE A CONTAINER

Pick a clean vase or jug which is taller than it is wide. Half fill it with water containing a cut flower preservative (see page 9)

STEP 2:
START TO MAKE THE TIED BUNCH

Conditioned flowers and foliage can be inserted directly into the water in the vase without any hand grouping beforehand (see below) but preparing a tied (or hand) bunch will often give a more pleasing effect. For best results the stems should be reasonably long and roughly the same thickness — all foliage which will be in water must be removed. You will need about 20 stems. Hold one of the longest ones between your thumb and forefinger — this will be the central pivot and the point of tying

STEP 3:
COMPLETE THE TIED BUNCH

Add further stems with each one at a slight angle — twist the bunch as you go. The heights of the flower-heads and foliage should decrease steadily as you progress, holding the tying point in your closed hand. Do not grip too tightly and the end result will be an all-round domed bunch. Tie at the central point with raffia or string

STEP 4:
PLACE THE BUNCH IN THE CONTAINER

Trim the base of the stems to the same level and insert in the vase or jug. If you have done the job correctly then the arrangement will fall open slightly to give a natural look. Fill with water to 1–2 in. (2.5–5 cm) below the rim

The Non-tied Bunch

The tied bunch is not for every situation. Soft-stemmed plants like Tulips and Daffodils can be damaged and an arrangement with woody stems and flowers is better created directly in the vase. To help hold the stems in place it is a good idea to add glass marbles or nuggets — in a glass vase they have a decorative effect and also hide the stem bases. Place the tallest stem first to form the central axis — other stems should be progressively shorter and appear to radiate from a point within the container. Use filler material to hide the edge of the vase.

Mechanics: FLORAL FOAM

Example: Line-mass Style — Crescent

STEP 1:
CHOOSE A CONTAINER

No other mechanics allow for such a wide choice of container — a shallow dish is suitable and so is a deep vase or urn. The basic provisos are that the vessel must be waterproof and that the top of the floral foam should be about 1 in. (2.5 cm) above the rim when it has been fixed in position. The most convenient type is the floral foam container which is designed to hold a rectangular or cylindrical block. This shallow plastic dish (page 11) calls for no additional support for the floral foam, and neither does a container in which a piece of foam has been cut and tightly wedged into the opening. In most cases, however, a container is chosen which is rather larger than the piece of floral foam and so is capable of acting as a water reservoir. This dish or bowl may be inserted into or taped onto a larger and more decorative container

STEP 2:
PREPARE THE FLORAL FOAM

The block of floral foam has usually to be cut to the required size — most people prefer to do this when the material is dry. Thorough wetting in water or dilute cut flower preservative solution is now necessary. A precise time for this operation cannot be given — it may take a minute or up to half an hour depending on the size of the block, water temperature etc. The best procedure is to lower the foam gently into a deep bowl of water and let go — do not push it down. It is ready when the top of the block has sunk to the water surface — take it out promptly as oversoaking leads to a loss of strength. Some arrangers cut ('chamfer') the edges of the block before creating an all-round arrangement

STEP 3:
PREPARE THE CONTAINER

This is easy with a floral foam container and a block cut to fit — simply push the foam into position. With other containers you will have to secure the block within the container, and using a frog (page 6) is the usual method. The container, frog and your hands must all be clean and dry — put 3 small blobs of kneaded adhesive clay ('fix') on the bottom of the frog and press it on to the base of the dish, bowl etc. Then push the floral foam on to the prongs until it is firmly held. This technique is not always practical — the inner surface of the container may be too shiny or else too valuable to spoil with adhesive clay. The answer here is to put a piece of damp tissue between the floral foam and the bottom of the container before strapping the block with adhesive tape, as shown in the illustration. Making a large arrangement calls for a modification of these instructions. You will need one big piece or several smaller blocks of foam taped together — 2 or more frogs will be required. Tape the blocks into the container and cover the surface with chicken wire which is then tucked into or strapped onto the rim

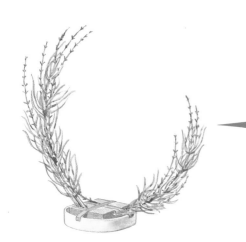

STEP 4:
INSERT LINE MATERIAL

A Crescent is an easy and effective arrangement to make. As noted on page 29 it does not call for a large amount of plant material, but the stems and flowers must be carefully chosen. The bold outline is provided by curved line material, and you will have to look for this in the garden or countryside. A smooth and regular arc is not essential — in fact many flower arrangers consider it undesirable. Look for naturally bent twigs on Forsythia, Quince, Ornamental Cherry, Pussy Willow, Dogwood etc. A number of whippy straight stems (Broom, Winter Jasmine, Rosemary and so on) can be curved by following the technique described for the Hogarth curve on page 29. Insert a long branch of line material in the top of the floral foam as shown — do not push stems more than 1 in. (2.5 cm) into the block. Balance this with a piece of stem in the side of the block at the other end. Repeat the process until a strong skewed crescent is formed. It is advisable to use more than one sort of line material — in the illustration Broom and Rosemary form the crescent

STEP 5:
INSERT DOMINANT MATERIAL

The arrangement so far has a firm and flowing shape but little interest. To provide a focal point it is necessary to add some dominant material which is usually a small group of eye-catching blooms — Rose, Paeony, Lily, Anthurium, Chrysanthemum, Gerbera, Orchid, Standard Carnation and Dahlia are examples. A pleasing effect is obtained by first grouping the largest dominant flowers close to the base of the arrangement. Then use some of the stems of this dominant material which bears opening flower buds — insert these stems so that they lie part way up the high curve, as shown in the illustration

STEP 6:
INSERT FILLER MATERIAL

The arrangement now has bold lines and a focal point, but two problems still remain. First of all, there is no softening between the line and dominant material, which is too 'modern' for many arrangers. Secondly, part of the mechanics and the container edge are exposed. The solution for these problems is to add some filler material — examples include leaves of Ivy, Hosta, Eucalyptus, Pittosporum, Conifer, Smoke Bush and small-bloomed flowers such as Gypsophila, Freesia and Alstroemeria. Soft and narrow stems are difficult to push into the foam — use a knitting needle or cocktail stick to make a hole for them. The arrangement is now finished, but look at it carefully before moving it to its chosen spot. A common mistake is to add excessive filler material which may obscure too much of the line material or detract from the focal point. Cut away any filler flowers or foliage which are making the display over-fussy, and consider putting a base under the container so as to improve the visual balance

Mechanics: CHICKEN WIRE

Example: Traditional Mass

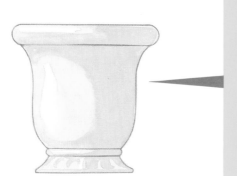

STEP 1:
CHOOSE A CONTAINER

The interest in chicken wire (wire netting) for holding plant stems in a flower arrangement declined sharply with the introduction of floral foam, and it has never recovered. There are, however, several situations where chicken wire remains the preferred mechanic — spring bulbs which find it difficult to take up water from foam, heavy stems and branches which require the support of rigid netting, and some tall plants such as Gladioli which prefer deep water to wet floral foam. For many floral decorators there are two additional virtues. Firstly, stems can be pulled out and reinserted at will until the desired result is obtained. In addition there is some plant movement as the arrangement is being created and this leads to a less stiff effect. The chosen container must be waterproof and the vase, jug or urn should be reasonably wide at the top

STEP 2:
PREPARE THE CHICKEN WIRE

Preparing a good chicken wire support is not as easy as it sounds — it calls for skill and experience. The basic features are firmness (you should be able to raise the container by lifting up the netting), good stem support (each shoot should pass through 3–4 layers of wire) and a fairly open centre (where most of the stems will be congregated). Use 2 in. (5 cm) mesh and cut a piece which is about twice the width and twice the depth of the container. Remove the thick edge and roll the netting into a loose ball. You are now ready to make the wire support within the container

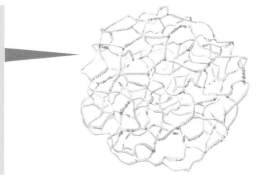

STEP 3:
PREPARE THE CONTAINER

Push part of the wire ball gently into the container — on no account should it be squashed down. Ease the ball down until the bottom touches the base of the vase or urn. Next, give the top a push so that a layer is formed near the base. Don't be heavy handed, and repeat the process until all the ball is within the container except for a dome of matted wire standing above the rim. If you have been successful then the crumpled meshes will still be large enough for you to be able to push a pencil through several layers — try it. Next, the chicken wire ball should be firm — it should not pull out if lifted. The final stage is to secure it with florist wire, rubber bands or tape. A satisfactory way is to weave adhesive tape through the top wire layer and then secure it to the sides of the container, as shown. Alternatively you may be able to secure the mechanics by bending the chicken wire edges over the rim of the pot. For a large and heavy arrangement some floral decorators place floral foam or a pinholder under the wire ball in the container. Now everything is in position and you are ready to start the arrangement

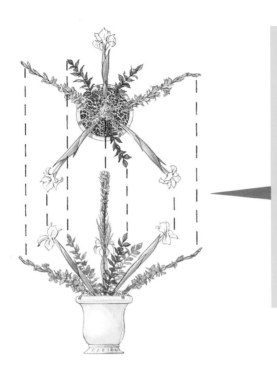

STEP 4:
INSERT LINE MATERIAL

Before you begin make sure that the leaves that would be in the container have all been removed, and half fill the vase or urn with dilute cut flower preservative solution. The first task is to establish the vertical axis — for this you will need one or more upright stems which are pushed down to the bottom of the container. The choice is large and it is up to you. There are leafy or coloured stems such as Dogwood, Beech, Privet, Elaeagnus, Butcher's Broom and Box. The choice with flowering stems is even greater — a few of the popular ones are Escallonia, Lily, Lilac, Forsythia, Camellia, Kniphofia, Rose, Quince, Foxtail Lily and Delphinium. The laterals forming the base of the display should be inserted after the vertical axis. Their length is usually about ⅔ of the vertical line material and 5 are used for a modest-sized arrangement — use 7 for a large display. These laterals can all be the same or different material — it's a matter of choice. Whatever you use, do make sure that the ends will be below the water surface. Finally, push in 3 stems of line material which will form the middle ribs of the display, as shown

STEP 5:
INSERT DOMINANT MATERIAL

The basic skeleton has been created and both the height and width of the display are now fixed. Within this boundary you have to place dominant flowers at intervals all round the arrangement — and that's where the skill comes in. A few hints. Don't just have one of anything — place several examples within the display. Next, group some of the flowers together rather than setting them all out singly. Cut the stems of the largest blooms so that the flowers will be set back in the arrangement and not standing on the outside, and place some of the dominant blooms near the top to ensure centres of interest at several levels

STEP 6:
INSERT FILLER MATERIAL

The arrangement is now spotted with a collection of eye-catching blooms which are separated by foliage or empty spaces. The final step is to reduce the contrasts by the use of filler material and this once again is a skilful task. Foliage is often important here, especially for covering the chicken wire, fastenings and the rim of the container. This foliage need not be plain green — you can use grey-leaved Senecio or Helichrysum, or variegated leaves such as Aucuba, Ivy and Euonymus. The choice of filler flowers, from the florist, garden and countryside is vast — old favourites include Solidago, Statice, Lady's Mantle, Hebe, Santolina, Mimosa, Gypsophila and Freesia. Don't forget the berried plants in winter — Skimmia, Holly, Pernettya, Snowberry etc. Finally, a few hints. Begin from the top and work downwards. Turn the arrangement as you work rather than trying to peer round the side, and remove some of the filler flowers and leaves if the arrangement looks overcrowded. The last task is to ensure that the water level is 1–2 in. (2.5–5 cm) below the rim

Mechanics: PINHOLDER

Example: Line Style — Ikebana

STEP 1:
CHOOSE A CONTAINER

A pinholder is an excellent way of securing heavy stems in a Line arrangement — it is of little use where a large number of thin stems are to be supported. The usual container is a shallow waterproof dish. If a tall container is to be used, partly fill with sand and then add a layer of melted candle wax. Push a shallow dish firmly into the wax and when set fix the pinholder as described below

STEP 2:
FIX THE PINHOLDER

The pinholder has to be fixed securely to the bottom of the dish. Place 3 small knobs of adhesive clay ('fix') to the bottom of the pinholder and press it down on to the dish. Pinholder, hands and dish must be clean and dry — protect your hands with a cloth or gloves if necessary. Position is a matter of personal choice — for Oriental arrangements it is often set off-centre. Half fill the dish with dilute cut flower preservative solution

STEP 3:
INSERT LINE MATERIAL

Gladiolus is featured in this example, but many other plants can be used such as Nandina, Forsythia, Flowering Cherry, Lily, Rosemary, Bamboo, Conifer, Heliconia and Rose. Woody stems should be cut at a sharp angle — cut soft stems straight across. Next, push the stem vertically on to or between the spikes. If the stem is to be set at an angle, hold the top of the stem with one hand and apply gentle but steady pressure with the other hand held just above the spikes. Push *away* from the sloping face, as shown. In this Moribana arrangement the taller stem (the Heaven line) is inserted first and then the shorter one (the Man line)

STEP 4:
FINISH THE ARRANGEMENT

The final step is to insert the Earth line — in this case a small group of Spider Chrysanthemums and Camellia leaves. Thin stems may need a 'shoe' (a small piece of thick stem into which the narrow shoot is inserted) before being pushed on to the spikes — alternatively you can wire several thin stems together. The pinholder can be covered with gravel if it is visible. Add sufficient cut flower preservative solution to ensure that all the stem bases are fully immersed

AFTERCARE

Aftercare begins as soon as the last flower or leafy stem has been put in place. The work involved calls for no skill and takes little effort, but failure to provide proper aftercare will result in the wilting and death of the floral material in a very short time. The benefits of proper aftercare are clearly shown in the series of photographs below.

The Rules of Aftercare

● TOP UP REGULARLY

Water is taken up at a surprisingly high rate, so it is usually necessary to top up the vase or dampen the floral foam every day. Use a long-spouted watering can and add water slowly and gently where space is restricted or foam is being moistened. Use drinking water or rainwater — do not use water which has been chemically softened. The water in the vase should not be changed unless it has become cloudy and evil-smelling.

● USE A CUT FLOWER PRESERVATIVE

A small amount of household bleach (see page 9) will help to kill the bacteria which contaminate the water and attack the cut ends of the stems. Proprietary preservatives generally contain a cut flower food (cane sugar) as well as a bacteriocide.

● PROTECT FROM HEAT & DRAUGHTS

Draughts cause excessive moisture loss, but are not as harmful as overheating. Keep your arrangement away from direct sunlight, radiators and open fires. The top of a TV set is not a good place for a floral display.

● KEEP AWAY FROM FRUIT

Do not place your arrangement close to a bowl of fruit. Apples, pears etc emit ethylene — a gas which accelerates the ripening of flowers.

● MIST OCCASIONALLY

Apply a mist-like spray above and around the arrangement once it has been placed in position. You can buy a trigger-operated mister at any garden centre, and it should be used regularly if the air is hot and dry. Do not spray close to delicate petals which may be damaged by water droplets.

● DEAD HEAD WHEN NECESSARY

The vase-life of one flower may be quite different from another species. Remove dead blooms promptly so that the display can continue to look attractive for several more days.

● STORE CONTAINER & MECHANICS

When the display is over both the container and metal mechanics (pinholder or chicken wire) should be washed thoroughly in soap and water before drying and storing. Keep moist floral foam wrapped in polythene.

Reviving Wilted Flowers

If some blooms have wilted it is often possible to revive them by cutting off an inch of stem under water and then using the 'wilted flower treatment' described on page 17. Once revived, return the stems to the arrangement as soon as possible.

GOOD AFTERCARE

Flower preservative added to vase water. Plants protected from draughts. Fine mist applied occasionally to blooms.

AFTER 0 DAYS AFTER 3 DAYS AFTER 8 DAYS

POOR AFTERCARE

Flower preservative not added to vase water. Plants not protected from draughts. Mist not applied to blooms.

AFTER 0 DAYS AFTER 3 DAYS AFTER 8 DAYS

CHAPTER 5

DRIED FLOWERS

Dried flower arrangements have been around for a long time — in 19th century homes they were to be found on pianos, sideboards and windowsills during the winter months when garden flowers were absent. Interest, however, waned as the 20th century householder regarded these stiff and often dusty bowls as a symbol of old-fashioned Victoriana. Twenty years ago it was difficult to buy more than a handful of different types of dried material.

Things have changed. Today you will find an extensive and varied collection of preserved plant material at any large florist or garden centre. No more is it just a matter of a few dried grasses, a small range of brown leaves or flowers and some sprigs of dried Lavender and Heather — with improved preservation techniques the colours are brighter and many spectacular shapes are available. Nor need you stick to shop-bought material — preserving home-grown and country-side plants will provide you with a free and abundant source of flowers and foliage for your displays.

So do set about making a dried flower arrangement if you have not done so before. You may have been discouraged by two drawbacks. The first one is that dried flowers do not have the natural appearance, natural colourings and short-lived beauty of fresh material. The answer here is not to regard them as rivals but to view them as partners in home display with rather different properties. The second drawback is the feeling that dried displays are drab and lifeless. This is because so many arrangements for sale in shops or on show in people's homes are indeed massed groups of little sprigs in brown, gold and cream which are crammed into wicker containers — the over-popular 'hedgehog in a basket'. This should not discourage you as this style is a hangover from earlier days. With the exciting materials now on sale and the new preservation techniques for home-grown leaves and flowers there is no reason why you cannot create modern eye-catching displays in a wide range of colours. Do read on and look at the examples of new-style dried flower arrangements on the following pages.

Having pointed out the two drawbacks, it is time to point out the advantages. Dried flower arrangements last for years and an occasional dusting is all the aftercare they need. Of course this permanence saves money as you do not have to keep buying fresh material if you rely on shop-bought material for your displays. It also saves time if flower arranging is not your hobby, as fresh arrangements have to be made all over again after a week or two and they do require regular topping-up with water. Two final advantages — the container need not be waterproof and the display need not be accessible as watering is not required.

Down to work with a number of practical points. First of all, the phrase 'dried flowers' is somewhat misleading. Some of the material is preserved in glycerine and is not dried, and much of it consists of leafy stems, seed-heads, large leaves, toadstools etc rather than flowers. The usual mechanic to hold the stems is brown floral foam, although setting and non-setting clay are occasionally used.

The chosen mechanic needs a container of some sort, and baskets have long been the favourite choice. But they are certainly not the only choice — for a Free-style or Abstract arrangement you will want to pick a less rustic container. A word of warning here. No water is added to the container which means that dried flower arrangements are light — to prevent the display from being knocked over partly fill a tall container with sand or gravel before making the arrangement.

Now for the plant material. The popular shop-bought types are illustrated on pages 53-55 and the garden plants which can be preserved in glycerine, silica gel or by air-drying are listed on pages 56-59. Oranges, creams and browns are the usual colours of air-dried plant material, but glycerine-treated foliage may be green or blue, and silica gel-treated blooms are quite bright. Brightest of all are the dyed leaves and flowers — brilliant blue, vivid red, glowing yellow and the rest. Their use is a matter of personal taste — for many flower arrangers a little goes a long way, but these bright artificial hues do have a place in modern settings.

As with fresh material you should follow the rules of good design described in Chapter 3. Do not always stick to Mass arrangements just because they dominate the displays seen in the shops. Line and Line-mass can be more exciting.

Buying Dried Plants

SOLIDASTER
(Solidaster)

PHLEUM
(Timothy Grass)

DELPHINIUM
(Larkspur)

IBERIS
(Candytuft)

HELIPTERUM
(Sunray)

LIMONIUM
(Rat's-tail Statice)

LIMONIUM
(Sea Lavender)

RUSCUS
(Butcher's Broom)

LIMONIUM
(Statice)

EUCALYPTUS
(Flat-leaf Eucalyptus)

HELICHRYSUM
(Straw Flower)

TANACETUM
(Tansy)

EUCALYPTUS
(Spiral Eucalyptus)

GOMPHRENA
(Globe Amaranth)

HYDRANGEA
(Hydrangea)

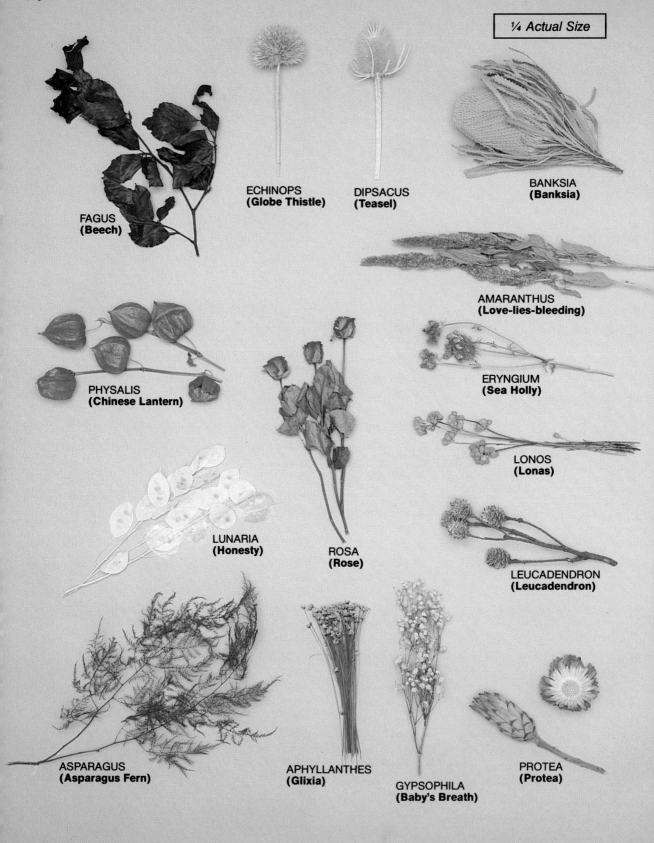

¼ Actual Size

ECHINOPS
(Globe Thistle)

DIPSACUS
(Teasel)

BANKSIA
(Banksia)

FAGUS
(Beech)

AMARANTHUS
(Love-lies-bleeding)

PHYSALIS
(Chinese Lantern)

ERYNGIUM
(Sea Holly)

LONOS
(Lonas)

LUNARIA
(Honesty)

ROSA
(Rose)

LEUCADENDRON
(Leucadendron)

ASPARAGUS
(Asparagus Fern)

APHYLLANTHES
(Glixia)

GYPSOPHILA
(Baby's Breath)

PROTEA
(Protea)

¼ Actual Size

**HORDEUM
(Barley)**

**TRITICUM
(Wheat)**

**AVENA
(Oat)**

**BRIZA
(Quaking Grass)**

**LAGURUS
(Bunny Tails)**

**PHALARIS
(Canary Grass)**

**NIGELLA DAMASCENA
(Love-in-a-mist)**

**NIGELLA ORIENTALIS
(Nigella orientalis)**

**CARTHAMUS
(Safflower)**

**ACHILLEA
(Yarrow)**

**PAPAVER
(Poppy)**

**NELUMBO
(Lotus)**

**LAVANDULA
(Lavender)**

**SILENE
(Campion)**

**HELIANTHUS
(Sunflower)**

Preserving Plants at Home

Many garden flowers, shrubs and trees as well as shop-bought cut flowers can be used to provide material for dried arrangements. There is no single method of preservation which is suitable for all plants. As a general rule air-drying is used for some flowers and seed-heads, and glycerine is chosen for foliage. Desiccants are recommended for showy blooms as the results are brighter and less crumpled than air-dried flowers. The quickest method and the one producing the most life-like dried flowers is silica gel in a microwave oven — see page 60. The lists in this section and in Chapter 11 will tell you which technique to use for the material you have chosen.

METHOD 1 : AIR-DRYING

● UPSIDE-DOWN DRYING

This is by far the most popular way of drying flowers. The secret of success is to find a place which is dark and comfortably warm — the airing cupboard is a favourite spot. Once dry the material can be arranged or stored away (see page 62).

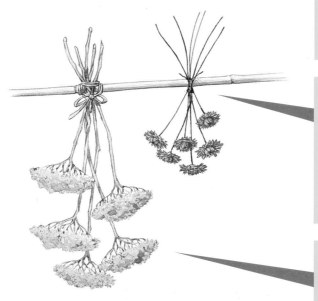

STEP 1:
CUT & PREPARE
THE MATERIAL
Pick a dry day and cut the blooms just before they are fully open. Seed-heads should be sprayed lightly with a hair lacquer aerosol. Remove the lower leaves and use absorbent paper to remove any surface moisture

STEP 2:
TIE THE STEMS TOGETHER
Tie the plants in bundles of 5–10 stems using string or raffia. Stagger the flowers or seed-heads so that they do not touch one another — see diagram. Wired flower-heads (page 61) should be grouped into bundles of 5–10 and then bound together with a wire tie — bend wires to separate the flower-heads

STEP 3:
HANG THE BUNDLES
UPSIDE DOWN
Choose a place which is dry, dark, airy and reasonably warm — all these conditions are important. Tie the bundles on a horizontal rod or wire — spread out the plants in each bundle so that air can circulate between the stems. Make sure that the bundles do not touch one another

STEP 4:
TAKE DOWN THE DRIED MATERIAL
Drying will take 1–8 weeks, depending on the species. Check at weekly intervals — make sure the ties are tight. The material is properly dried when it is crisp all over — remove as soon as this stage is reached

Plants suitable for Upside-down Drying

ACANTHUS	CENTAUREA	GAILLARDIA	PHYSALIS
ACHILLEA	CLARKIA	HELICHRYSUM	RANUNCULUS
ALCHEMILLA	CLEMATIS	LAVANDULA	SALVIA
AMARANTHUS	DAHLIA	LIATRIS	SANTOLINA
ANAPHALIS	DELPHINIUM	LIMONIUM	SENECIO
ASTILBE	ECHINOPS	LUNARIA	SOLIDAGO
ASTRANTIA	ERICA	NIGELLA	TRITICUM
CALENDULA	ERYNGIUM	PAPAVER	XERANTHEMUM

● UPRIGHT DRYING

Some plants dry better if stood upright rather than being hung upside down — the notable examples are Hydrangea and the prominent seed-pod types such as Lunaria (Honesty). Water is added to the container holding the stems — this water is absorbed and the plants benefit from the slow drying process which results.

STEP 1:
CUT & PREPARE
THE MATERIAL
Follow Step 1 on page 56 for Upside-down Drying. With Hydrangea you should wait until the flowers are papery dry on the plant before cutting

STEP 2:
PLACE THE STEMS
IN A CONTAINER
Choose a container which will hold the stems upright during the drying process. Add about 1 in. (2.5 cm) of water to the vase, jug or bottle and then put in the plants. As with Upside-down Drying the place chosen for the container should be dry, dark, airy and reasonably warm

STEP 3:
REMOVE THE DRIED MATERIAL
Check at weekly intervals. If all the water has gone and the plants are crisp and dry, they should be removed for arranging or storage. If they are still limp then add a little more water until the dry container/ crisp plant stage is reached

Plants suitable for Upright Drying

ACACIA	ANAPHALIS	GYPSOPHILA	MOLUCELLA
ACHILLEA	DAHLIA	HYDRANGEA	ROSA
AMARANTHUS	DELPHINIUM	LUNARIA	SANTOLINA

● FLAT DRYING

Leaves, feathery grasses and heavy seed-heads are best dried flat on absorbent paper — make a support frame of chicken wire and cover the surface with paper towels.

STEP 1:
CUT & PREPARE
THE MATERIAL
As with all drying methods the plants should be dry at the time of cutting. Midsummer is the best time for deciduous leafy material — any time of the year will do for evergreens

STEP 2:
PLACE THE STEMS
ON ABSORBENT PAPER
Lay leafy branches and grasses on the paper — make sure that the plants are not touching each other as proper air circulation is vital. Heavy seed-heads are best cut with a short stem which is then pushed through the paper. Keep in a dry, dark, airy and reasonably warm place

STEP 3:
REMOVE THE
DRIED MATERIAL
Check at weekly intervals until the dry and crisp stage is reached — change the paper if it is damp. With large and fleshy seed-heads this may take a couple of months. When the material is crisp all over it should be removed for arrangement or storage

Plants suitable for Flat Drying

ALLIUM	CORTADERIA	HOSTA	PROTEA
BRIZA	CYNARA	LAVANDULA	ZEA

METHOD 2 : DESICCANTS

A desiccant is a fine-grained material which readily absorbs moisture — when placed in close contact with a flower or leaf the drying process is quicker than leaving the plant to dry in a dark, airy room. The use of a desiccant is not only a quicker process than air-drying — it also ensures that much more of the colour and original shape of the bloom are retained, and with some flowers the fragrance remains. Still, there are a few drawbacks. The desiccant has to be paid for and its use is a much more fiddly business than simply hanging up plants to dry. The most serious drawback is that the stems become very brittle, which means that the flowers or seed-heads have to be wired either before or after drying. These are undoubtedly disadvantages, but if you want your dried blooms to look as life-like as possible, then desiccants are the only well-established answer.

A number of different materials have been used over the years. Washed fine sand is the cheapest, but it is heavy and slow-acting. Alum and borax were once popular, but they sometimes give disappointing results. The best desiccant is undoubtedly silica gel as it works in just a few days, thereby ensuring maximum shape and colour retention. The grade to use is the horticultural one sold for drying flowers — it contains a moisture indicator which is blue when dry and turns pink when moisture has been absorbed.

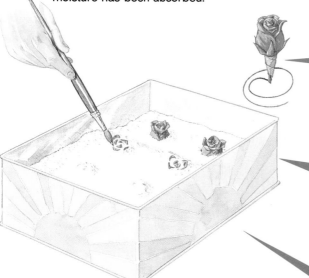

STEP 1:
CUT & PREPARE THE MATERIAL
Pick a dry day and cut the blooms before they are fully open — ripe flowers will shed their petals when dried. It will be necessary to create artificial stems after the flowers have been dried, so you should cut the stalks to leave a 1 in. (2.5 cm) stem. Attach a piece of wire (see page 61 for details) and coil it below the flower as shown

STEP 2:
PREPARE THE CONTAINER
You will need a lidded air-tight container — use a separate one (biscuit tin, plastic freezer box or ice-cream container) for each type of flower to be dried. Dry the silica gel unless it is new and in a sealed bag — place it on a baking tray in a warm oven for about an hour. Pour a 2 in. (5 cm) layer into the dry container

STEP 4:
TAKE OUT THE DRIED MATERIAL
Open the box and gently dig out one of the flowers with a slotted spoon after 2 days. Small blooms should be dry at this stage — if the petals are paper-crisp then take out all the flowers with the spoon and remove any adhering grains with a paintbrush. If the test flower is not fully dry then return it to the silica gel and reseal the container. Examine daily — some large blooms may take up to 5 days to dry. A word of warning — remove the blooms as soon as they are dry as prolonging the treatment will make them very brittle. Keep the silica gel for future use

STEP 3:
PUT THE FLOWERS IN THE CONTAINER
Gently push the wired stems into the silica gel so that the blooms are upright and not touching. Next, gently sprinkle the desiccant over and around the flowers. It is essential that all parts are covered, which means that a soft paintbrush should be used to work the grains between the petals — use a toothpick if necessary. Shake the box occasionally. Finally, cover the flowers with a ½ in. (1 cm) layer of silica gel and put the lid on tightly

Plants suitable for Desiccant Drying

ALSTROEMERIA	DAHLIA	LILIUM	RANUNCULUS
ANEMONE	DELPHINIUM	MAGNOLIA	ROSA
CALENDULA	DIANTHUS	MATTHIOLA	RUDBECKIA
CAMELLIA	FREESIA	MIMOSA	SCABIOSA
CHEIRANTHUS	GERBERA	MUSCARI	SILVERY FOLIAGE
CHRYSANTHEMUM	HELLEBORUS	NARCISSUS	TULIPA
CLEMATIS	IBERIS	PAEONY	VIOLA
CONVALLARIA	LATHYRUS	PRIMULA	ZINNIA

METHOD 3 : GLYCERINE

Glycerine treatment is not a way of drying plant material — it preserves foliage and a few flower-heads by replacing the water in the tissues. The preserved leaves are quite pliable and will last for years if properly stored. The usual colour is a shade of brown, ranging from the creamy tones of Box to the dark chocolate of Rhododendron. Brown is not the only colour — Eucalyptus turns blue-green and both Rose and Beech may be dark green or brown when preserved, depending on the time of year and variety. This technique is generally used for leafy stems or large individual leaves and the preserved foliage is extremely useful in floral decoration. It can be used in fresh arrangements — merely wipe the base of the stems and allow to dry after use. It can also be used in dried arrangements to provide bold line material.

● UPRIGHT PRESERVING

STEP 1:
CUT & PREPARE THE MATERIAL

Cut, pre-condition and condition the plants as for a fresh flower arrangement — see pages 16–17. Make sure that lower and all damaged leaves have been removed, the foliage has been washed and the stem bases cut diagonally. Evergreens can be preserved at any time — deciduous material should be cut in midsummer

STEP 2:
PLACE THE STEMS IN GLYCERINE SOLUTION

Choose a container which is large enough to hold the stems upright — if the stems are tall it may be necessary to stand the container in a bucket. Thoroughly mix 1 part of glycerine with 2 parts of near-boiling water — pour some into the container and insert the stems so that they are standing in about 3 in. (7.5 cm) of liquid. Keep in a cool and shady place

STEP 3:
TAKE OUT THE PRESERVED MATERIAL

Inspect the plants at weekly intervals — the upper leaves on long stems should be wiped occasionally with a cloth soaked in the glycerine solution. It is time to remove the stems when all the leaves have changed colour — there is no need to wait until drops of glycerine begin to ooze out on to the leaf surface. The preserving process will take 1–8 weeks depending on the plant — top up the solution as necessary. Pat dry with a paper towel and either store or place in a flower arrangement. If possible hang upside down for a few days before use

Plants suitable for Upright Preserving

BUXUS	EUCALYPTUS	MAGNOLIA	QUERCUS
CAMELLIA	FAGUS	MAHONIA	RHODODENDRON
CHOISYA	FERNS	MOLUCELLA (+ flowers)	ROSA
COTONEASTER	GARRYA (+ catkins)	PITTOSPORUM	ROSMARINUS
CYTISUS	HYDRANGEA (+ flowers)	PRUNUS (evergreen)	SALIX
ELAEAGNUS	ILEX (+ berries)	PYRUS	SORBUS

● FLAT PRESERVING

STEP 1:
PLACE THE LEAVES IN GLYCERINE SOLUTION
Large leaves or sprays of smaller ones can be preserved singly by partly filling a large dish with glycerine solution and then immersing the foliage in the liquid. Some experts recommend a stronger solution than the upright preserving one — 1 part glycerine to 1 part near-boiling water

STEP 2:
TAKE OUT THE PRESERVED MATERIAL
Some leaves will take longer than others. A leaf is ready when it has changed colour all over — it is now time to take it out of the glycerine solution. It will be sticky, so wash it thoroughly and then dab with a paper towel to dry. When fully dry it is ready for arranging or storage (see page 62)

Plants suitable for Flat Preserving

ACANTHUS
ASPIDISTRA
AUCUBA
BERGENIA
FATSIA
FICUS
HEDERA
HOSTA

METHOD 4 : SKELETONISING

Skeletonised leaves are available from some larger florists and garden centres, providing unusual material to serve as an attractive background feature in floral arrangements. Unfortunately it is not easy to find a supplier and the range of shapes is limited. Obviously a do-it-yourself technique would be useful, but most experts regard skeletonising as a job for the professionals. However, with patience and a little luck you can produce these leaves at home.

You may be lucky enough to find naturally-skeletonised leaves half-buried in the debris beneath the branches of Camellia, Holly or Rhododendron, but it is usually necessary to start from scratch. Choose large leaves — Oak, Camellia, Laurel, Maple, Rhododendron and Magnolia are suitable subjects. The leaves should be free from blemishes — they should be mature and healthy. Stir a handful of washing soda in a large enamel saucepan half-filled with soft water and boil the leaves for about an hour. Put on rubber or plastic gloves and remove one leaf to see if you can rub off some of the soft green tissue under a running tap. If the soft tissue is still firmly attached, continue the boiling process for another hour.

Remove the leaves one at a time. Lay each one in turn on a piece of absorbent paper and scrape off all the soft tissue with the back of a knife. Rinse under a running tap and repeat the process until a clean leaf skeleton is obtained. Do not remove the next leaf from the soda solution until you have properly skeletonised the first one. Soak each skeletonised leaf in dilute bleach and then spread them on absorbent paper to dry. For curled leaves wrap around a pencil or candle. After a day or two they will be ready. The leaf stem will be weak and will have to be wired for support. Now you have your own home-made skeletonised leaves.

METHOD 5 : MICROWAVING

The microwave adds a new dimension to preserving flowers and sprigs of silver or grey foliage. No other method can match it for colour retention or speed — the whole process takes a matter of minutes. It is therefore extremely surprising that so little has been written on the subject. Home microwave drying is still in its infancy and there are no clear-cut and generally-agreed rules as there are for air-drying and glycerine. Microwave drying is strictly for the experimentally-minded. You will no doubt have some disappointments but with garden flowers it doesn't matter as you can try again in a few minutes. Do keep a record of settings and times for your successes.

The easier technique is **Open Drying** — merely arrange the flowering stems in rows on a few layers of absorbent paper in the microwave. Switch on at half-power for 2–3 minutes and then hang the stems upside-down for a couple of days if you do not plan to use them immediately. This technique is suitable for plants with a mass of small flowers, such as Gypsophila, Alchemilla, Solidago and Lavender. You must condition the stems (see pages 16–17) before drying.

Silica-gel Drying is more complex, but large-flowered types such as Rose, Anemone, Viola, Tulip and Chrysanthemum can be tackled. Follow the silica-gel technique (page 58) with two important exceptions — the plant material must be conditioned (pages 16–17) before placing in the desiccant so that the tissues are full of water, and wiring of the flower-heads should take place *after* drying. The container must be microwave-compatible. Put a cup half-filled with water in the microwave alongside the container and switch on at full power for 1–3 minutes — remove the flowers after about 30 minutes standing time.

Wiring

If your arrangements use only fresh plants then you may never have to bother with wiring unless you wish to hold up a floppy stem or heavy flower- or seed-head. The wiring of fresh arrangements is part of floristry rather than flower arranging. The situation is different with dried flowers. Here the stems may have to be lengthened, strengthened or replaced, and wiring is an important technique to learn, especially if you dry your own plants.

SUPPORT FOR A FRESH STEM

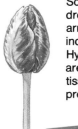

Some flower stems are inclined to droop quite quickly, making the arrangement unsightly. Examples include Anemone, Tulip, Ranunculus, Hyacinth and Larkspur. Such stems are either hollow or made up of soft tissue, and wiring can be used to provide support.

Insert a length of stub wire (see page 9) into the base of the stem. Push gently and steadily upwards, taking care not to pierce the side. Stop when the base of the flower is reached

FALSE STEM BEFORE DRYING

It is usually easier to wire stemless or short-stemmed flowers before rather than after drying. Some, such as Helichrysum, should always be wired before drying in silica gel.

Insert a length of stub wire through the base of the flower. Bend the tip into a U-shaped loop, as shown. Now pull the wire back until the top of the loop is hidden within the heart of the flower

BUNCHING

Dried sprigs of plants with small flowers are often easier to arrange than single stems. Use medium-gauge stub wire for bunching.

Arrange the group of stems so that the cut ends are level. Place a length of stub wire alongside the parallel stems so that its end is level with the bottom of the stems. Now bend the wire at the desired maximum height of the binding and then wind the wire downwards. Cut off the excess wire when the stem ends are reached

FALSE STEM AFTER DRYING

Flowers dried in silica gel are often left with a 1-2 in. (2.5-5 cm) stem. After drying, this short stem should be bound to a medium- or heavy-gauge stub wire, as shown.

Place and hold a length of stub wire next to the short stalk and bind them both together with fine rose wire. Large flower- or seed-heads such as Protea, Helianthus etc will have to be bound to a thin cane by means of stub wire

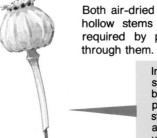

Both air-dried and glycerine-treated hollow stems can be extended if required by pushing a stub wire through them.

Insert a length of stub wire into the base of the dried or preserved hollow stem. Push gently and steadily upwards, taking care not to pierce the side

COVER FOR A FALSE STEM

False stems of wire or wired cane should be covered if they will be visible in the finished arrangement. Floral tape (see page 9) is used for this purpose — choose green or brown as appropriate.

Press the end of the floral tape around the base of the flower. Turn the false stem steadily with one hand while holding the tape at an angle with the other. Make sure the floral tape overlaps so that the wire or cane is fully hidden. Stop when the end of the false stem is reached. Cut the tape — seal and smooth the end and sides of the covered false stem with your fingers

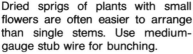

Colouring

Dyes and aerosol paints are available for colouring fresh flowers and leaves, but their use is generally frowned upon by experts and purists. Nature doesn't really need a helping hand, but there is no reason why you should not occasionally produce novelty flowers for an arrangement. This calls for immersing the flower stalks in a dye solution before making the display. Use a food dye — choose a strong colour and a large white or pastel bloom. Dissolve 1 fl.oz (30 ml) in 1 pint (approx. ½ litre) of warm water — add 1 teaspoon of sugar. Immerse the stalks in about 3 in. (7.5 cm) of liquid — remove when the desired colour has been achieved. This will take 1–24 hours after which the ends should be washed under running water and then re-cut. All the petal surface or just the veins will be distinctly coloured — an attractive or bizarre effect, depending on your point of view.

The situation is different with dried or preserved flowers, as Nature sometimes does need a helping hand with this material. Perhaps the most acceptable technique is to add a few drops of green floral dye when preserving Eucalyptus, Beech etc in glycerine. The aim should be to strengthen natural colours rather than to produce distinctly artificial hues. Another technique is to dip plant material which is a dull brown into a dilute household bleach solution until it changes to an attractive cream colour. Wash, dab with absorbent paper and hang up to dry. A more natural way to bleach dried plants is to place them in a sunny window.

You will find masses of dip-dyed material at any large florist. Flower dyes are available if you want to do your own — the plant material is immersed in a solution of the dye, after which it is dab-dried with absorbent paper and then hung to dry. Be careful here — vivid reds and blues can be hard to place in an arrangement.

Spray-painting dried material with a floral aerosol is another possibility. This is not often done for much of the year but it comes into its own at Christmastime, when vast quantities of Holly, Conifer sprigs, dried Wheat etc are sprayed with gold or silver paint before being placed in wreaths, swags or baskets.

Storing

Most dried and preserved plants are prepared during the summer months, which is the time when we are busy with fresh flower arrangements. It is therefore necessary to store much of the dried material for later use. Leaving it to hang in the dark cupboard where it was dried is usually ideal, but the space can rarely be spared. A long-established method is to hang the bunches in the kitchen for both decoration and storage. Unfortunately this may not be practical in the average-sized modern house, and as a technique the light and moist conditions in a kitchen shorten the life and bleach the colour of dried plants.

You need a dark and dry place for storage, and the best solution is a cardboard box — a flower box from a florist for long-stemmed types and a shoe box for smaller specimens. Both dried and glycerined plants are stored in the same way — but *never* in the same box. Another word of caution — never use plastic bags for storage.

Before you start, make sure the plants are really dry. It is a good idea to lightly spray flower- and seed-heads with a hair lacquer or acrylic sealer. Tie the plants into loose bundles and place at the bottom of the box to form the first level — use the heaviest-headed plants for this purpose. Next place a second layer, making sure that one group of heads does not lay directly over heads in the layer below. Provide further protection by placing tissue or absorbent kitchen paper below the flower- or seed-heads. Delicate plants are sometimes wrapped individually or in groups in newspaper before packing. Replace the lid and store in a dry place. You may find that some of the flowers are rather crushed when taken out of the box — revive them by holding them in steam and then dressing the petals with a brush or stick as necessary.

The **MASS** Style

◁ *A relatively new concept which has not yet gained widespread popularity. A wicker basket is filled with dry floral foam — flower-heads are then inserted to form a patterned carpet. Names used for this type of display include Tapestry, Carpet Bed and Shadow Box.*

Modern Mass is frequently seen in quality house ▷ *magazines and in fashionable florist shops, but has not become popular with the general public. In its standard form a single plant type is displayed in a basket — see page 73. On this page the more colourful Stepped Mass arrangement is shown — various dried plants are placed at different levels.*

◁ *The Traditional Mass arrangement made with dried flowers is usually the 'Hedgehog'. Spines of line material radiate from the box or basket and the spaces in between are almost entirely filled with a range of dried blooms. Can be interesting, but is often dull.*

The LINE Style

A Marian Aaronson piece of Abstract sculpture. The dried husks from a large S. African Aloe have been placed on and alongside a metal ring holder. Truly dramatic, but it is art rather than flower arranging. ▷

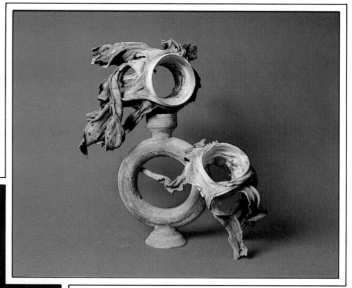

◁ This Free-style display by Marian Aaronson is truly a flower arrangement, unlike her Abstract creation above. The round heads of Allium giganteum were impaled on lively curved stems above a cleverly crafted vase.

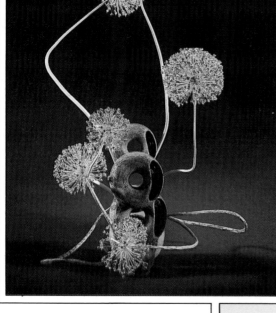

This is a Free-style rather than an Abstract arrangement as both foliage and flowers are in their dried natural form. The dominant features, however, of this exhibition display are the vertical wooden stake and the tree trunk section. ▷

◁ *Dried flower arrangements need not be creamy and brown like a field of Wheat nor garishly coloured with dyed material. This charming display could be mistaken for a fresh arrangement. The flowers were dried using the silica gel/microwave technique (page 60) and the Eucalyptus was glycerine-treated.*

This display is the Line-mass version of the 'Hedgehog' arrangement illustrated on page 63. Once again the heart of the display is a mass of material, but above it is a widely-spaced fan of straight-stemmed line material. ▷

◁ *A small display in which a strong and flowing line rises above the massed collection below. The colours are muted. Air-dried material has been used and the dominant flowers are Achillea millefolium and Nigella damascena.*

The MISCELLANEOUS Style

The Parallel arrangement is set to ▷
become increasingly popular and it is
an excellent way of using preserved
flowers and foliage. Pictured here is a
good example by Gill McGregor —
note the wide range of shapes and
textures which have been used.

◁ It is not a good idea to create a Garland with
fresh flowers as this type of arrangement is
quite fiddly to make and vase-life is short. It is
better to use dried flowers and glycerine-
preserved foliage as illustrated here.

Plaques made with dried material are a ▷
useful form of wall decoration — the
3-D effect provides a welcome change
from paintings and photographs. Very
often the backboard is plain — in this
example it is an integral part of the
display.

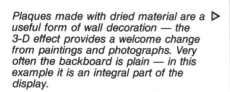

CHAPTER 6
ARTIFICIAL FLOWERS

Artificial flowers are not new — the Ancient Chinese and Greeks fashioned foliage and blooms in gold and porcelain. For centuries there have been flowers made out of pottery, enamelled metal, feathers, parchment and many other materials, but not until quite recently were they designed to be arranged in a bowl or vase. The first artificials for arranging were crafted out of paper — plain or treated and then painted. The best of them were works of art and far too expensive for ordinary everyday use. The popular revolution began about 30 years ago when moulded plastic flowers flooded in from the Far East. They were cheap enough to be used occasionally as promotional giveaways, but were generally not good enough for serious flower arranging. Their heyday is past, but plastic Conifer branches are still used in wreaths at Christmastime, and so are gold-sprayed plastic Poinsettias. It was the arrival of the 'silk' flower which brought artificials into the world of flower arranging. The material used is woven polyester fibre, although the terms 'silk' and 'designer' flowers are used for blooms made from pure silk, latex and parchment as well as polyester. An extensive range can be found in garden centres, florists, department stores and other outlets these days, and even the experts are occasionally fooled into thinking that they are real flowers at first glance. The artificial bloom generally sets out to imitate a freshly-cut one, but artificial dried material with slightly crumpled blooms and brown foliage is becoming increasingly popular. The stems of silk flowers are made of plastic, plastic-coated wire or wire covered with floral tape.

They are put to various uses. An arrangement made solely of artificial flowers is the obvious choice when a display with bright and real-looking blooms is required in a situation where permanence is a prime requirement or where watering is impossible. Artificial blooms are sometimes used to brighten up dried flower arrangements — if used in a fresh flower display you should paint any exposed wire stem bases with nail polish before placing in water or wet floral foam.

You have read this introduction and you have no doubt seen many examples of silk flowers in the shops, and you will have to decide whether you find them acceptable. Some flower arrangers will not use them — for these people a floral display is Nature brought indoors. Other flower arrangers feel that the restrained use of artificial blooms can sometimes be employed to add colour to a dried flower arrangement, or to produce wholly artificial displays in hard-to-reach situations.

If you decide to use silk flowers, then do follow the rules to get the best out of them. The first rule is that you should buy the best — this material is expensive, but it is much better to buy just a few stems of life-like flowers than to purchase a mass of cheap 'flowers' which wouldn't fool anyone. Next, don't get carried away by the large exotics, even if you can afford them. They do have a place, especially in the Grand arrangement, but small and more subdued material is usually easier to fit into an arrangement, and may be less obviously false.

Use brown floral foam or wire netting as you would do for a dried flower arrangement. You can save money and add a more natural look at the same time by incorporating some dried or preserved foliage from your own garden. Do try for seasonal arrangements even though the material is permanent — Daffodils and Tulips in late summer make it so obvious that the plants are not real.

If the stems are too long, it is usually better to bend them over before inserting rather than to cut them, as you may need the extra length in the next arrangement you make. Do flick over the petals and leaves with a feather duster occasionally, as grime is the main enemy. Polyester flowers can be washed by dipping them into warm water with a little detergent added and then rinsing by dipping into plain water — be careful not to wet the mechanics. Despite the everlasting nature of the material there will probably come a time when you are tired of the display — simply dismantle it in the usual way and store the artificial material in plastic bags.

Buying Artificial Flowers

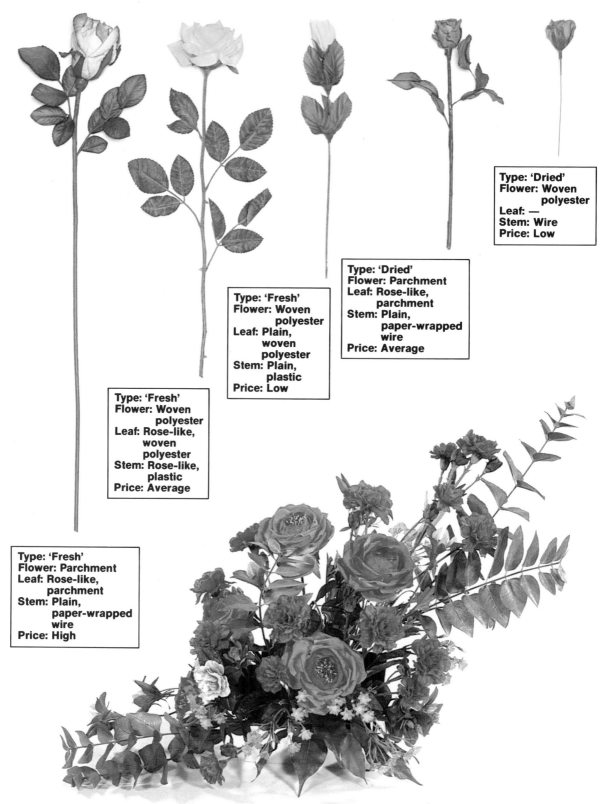

Type: 'Dried'
Flower: Woven
      polyester
Leaf: —
Stem: Wire
Price: Low

Type: 'Dried'
Flower: Parchment
Leaf: Rose-like,
      parchment
Stem: Plain,
      paper-wrapped
      wire
Price: Average

Type: 'Fresh'
Flower: Woven
      polyester
Leaf: Plain,
      woven
      polyester
Stem: Plain,
      plastic
Price: Low

Type: 'Fresh'
Flower: Woven
      polyester
Leaf: Rose-like,
      woven
      polyester
Stem: Rose-like,
      plastic
Price: Average

Type: 'Fresh'
Flower: Parchment
Leaf: Rose-like,
      parchment
Stem: Plain,
      paper-wrapped
      wire
Price: High

CHAPTER 7

ARRANGEMENTS AROUND THE HOUSE

The fascination of having plants around us is a fact which everybody knows but nobody can really explain. We enjoy them in the garden, park and countryside and we want them in our home. There are two basic ways to do so — we can have pots of living house plants in soil or compost, or we can have arrangements of freshly cut, dried or artificial flowers and foliage in water, floral foam or clay. This is not really an either/or situation — most of us choose to have examples of both types in one or more rooms in the place where we live.

We have to accept that the fresh floral arrangement lacks the permanence of a house plant, and the dried display is not actually alive and growing like an African Violet or Rubber Plant. But the floral arrangement does have two distinct advantages over the pot plant. The material is free for the taking from the garden or hedgerow, and the making of the display allows the arranger to be creative — to exercise skill, judgement and artistic ability. There are six basic sites for floral arrangements around the house or apartment — these are the rooms or areas where you may find one or more displays of cut or dried flowers. Note the use of the word 'may' and not 'will'. It would be an unusual living room which did not have at least one arrangement or display during the year, but it would be equally rare to find a house which has a fresh arrangement throughout the year in the bathroom. So the use of individual rooms as display points varies quite markedly, and so does the role of the arrangement. It may serve as a focal point or a centre of interest which is not at all uncommon in an entrance hall, or it may serve merely as a small part in the overall decoration of the room, as in the kitchen.

This book so far has guided you through the pathways of ingredients, styles and features of good design to the spot where even the first-time arranger can make a reasonably attractive display. Now it is decision time — which is the best room for the display you have just made or alternatively what is the right sort of display to make for the room you have in mind? Should you make one impressive display or a series of small ones to put on side tables?

Previous chapters have been peppered with rules, and sometimes precise rules concerning conditioning, use of mechanics, drying techniques and so on. Here, however, there are no rules — the choice of style, material etc for a particular room is up to you. The fundamental principle is that a good arrangement is one which pleases you and the family. This may be a small cluster of opening Rose buds in a glass dish for the traditionalist or a large ball of barbed wire on top of a bamboo trunk for the avant-garde. Neither is 'good' nor 'bad' — it is just a matter of personal taste.

There are a number of guidelines which are generally accepted as sound practice and which you can choose to follow or ignore. The first one is that an arrangement is most satisfying when the container, plant material and style are in keeping with the character and decor of the room. Masses of cottage-garden plants in jugs or earthenware bowls will add colour and charm to a chintzy living room, but the stark and simple lines of a modern living area would be more comfortable with a Free-style, Abstract or Modern mass arrangement. The next guideline is to remember that there are other supports than the table, sideboard and windowsill for floral arrangements. There are the wall for wreaths, swags and hanging containers, the floor for fireplace displays and the pedestal to display an arrangement with pendent festoons of foliage and flowers. Next, there are a number of purely practical considerations. Don't have tall glass containers where toddlers can knock them over, and think of a wall display rather than a side table one in a narrow hall where space is strictly limited. The remaining guidelines are controversial and not everyone will agree. Firstly, having a number of similar-sized arrangements in similar styles can look monotonous, and if made in completely different materials can look 'bitty'. From the design point of view it is better to have one major display and then one or more subsidiary ones which have some degree of linkage in material, container or style. Secondly, don't overdo it. This may seem strange advice in a book which unashamedly sets out to increase your interest in flower arranging, but your home is not a florist shop and should not be made to look like one. Having displays all over the place will diminish the impact of the really good arrangement which should be a centre of interest.

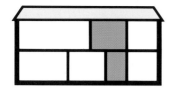

The Hall/Landing

The entrance hall is an excellent site for a flower arrangement. It is here that the visitors gain their first impression of your home, and there are few things which can match the ability of a collection of flowers to transform the hall from a dark and uninviting place into a lively and welcoming one. You can use flowering pot plants or a floral arrangement for this display, and do think about the conditions before making your choice. Poor light and cold nights severely limit the house plants you can use, but these factors are not a problem for an arrangement made with fresh or dried plant material.

Nobody stands for long in the hall, so the display should be eye-catching enough to make an immediate impression. Unfortunately most halls are long, cramped and narrow, which means that you probably cannot create this eye-catching effect with grandeur. You must rely instead on bold colour or a distinctive shape to make a wall, windowsill or side table display interesting. A couple of precautions. Firstly, make sure that the container is heavy or low enough and the plant material restricted enough to prevent the display from being knocked over by running children or clumsy visitors. Secondly, remember that a large display in a small hall will make it look smaller.

Of course these restrictions do not apply if you have a spacious hall. Here is the place for the pedestal or polished table bearing a really expansive and colourful display to welcome the visitor. Fresh flowers wherever possible — leave the dried and artificial displays for more difficult and less important places around the house.

The landing at the top of the stairs is often the barest spot in the home. Do consider a bright arrangement here — dried or fresh depending on the season and your own preference.

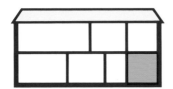

The Kitchen

The kitchen is second only to the living room as the most popular place for house plants — more than half have at least one on the windowsill or by a work surface. Most of these pot-grown specimens appreciate the moist air, and water for keeping the compost damp is readily to hand. Flower arrangements are much less of a feature in the kitchen — there is often not the space for the type of display we create for the living room. The kitchen is often regarded as a work area, and however irrational it may be we want a living area for the display we have created, and so the first choice is the living or dining room. In the same way we hang our pictures in these rooms rather than the kitchen.

However, much of the day is often spent in the kitchen, and flowers help to bring the garden indoors. The house plant display is so often one of green leaves rather than bright blooms, and so one should consider the kitchen for a flower arrangement even if space is limited. This is the place for a compact and casual seasonal arrangement — Daffodils in spring, Roses in summer and berries plus coloured leaves in autumn. Nothing too grand — a tied bunch in a vase (page 21) is excellent. The experts advise that the container should be in keeping with the food/kitchen image — an enamel pot, old kettle, earthenware jug etc. This is right for the traditional kitchen but a little out of place in a modern stainless-steel one. Dried flower arrangements are not a good idea as many varieties deteriorate quite quickly in steamy air, but a display of upside-down bunches of the more tolerant sorts (see page 75) has long been a feature of country kitchens. If you live in an apartment then you will not be able to go into the garden to pick a few spring flowers or Roses to pop into a jug. Buying florist flowers for this purpose may be too costly for you, so it is worth considering a small display of artificial flowers to brighten up a dull area of this important room.

The Living Room

It is not surprising that the living room is chosen as the prime site for the showiest flower displays. Making an arrangement is extremely satisfying, but it is equally important to enjoy the display once it has been created. This means putting it in a place where we can relax and look at our handiwork, and the living room is the one spot in the home where we do have time to sit and look around. It is also the room where the family gathers and friends sit with their coffee cups, and so displays here get more than a casual glance. This means that it has to be a place for our best work — mechanics must be completely hidden and later on arrangements must be broken up before the flowers droop and shrivel.

The living room consists of a number of recommended plant stations which can be used to house floral displays. The open fireplace between spring and autumn is a key focal point — a dried flower arrangement in keeping with the size and style of the surround is an important design feature in the living room. Windows are also important — a windowsill arrangement links the garden with the room. Unfortunately a sunny window is not a plant-friendly spot — fresh flowers quickly reach maturity and dried material is bleached. A bare corner is an excellent spot for a floor-standing or table-borne display — Modern mass, large Symmetrical triangle, Traditional mass and Topiary trees are some of the favourite styles for this plant station. At the other end of the scale are the side table displays — here the object is to create attractive arrangements which are compact enough not to get in the way. Several places are fine for dried or artificial flower arrangements but not for fresh ones — the mantelpiece above a roaring fire, a high shelf or the top of the TV are examples. A final word of caution — don't try to fill every potential plant station with floral arrangements. House plants will undoubtedly be a good choice for one or more places in this room and will provide a permanent and living green backcloth to complement your colourful floral creations.

◁ The fireplace is often the focal point in the living room. The large fireplace in the grand room calls for a bold dried arrangement from spring until autumn. An impressive Fan, perhaps, or a modern Parallel display as illustrated here.

The modest fireplace can be brightened up with ▷ a dried flower arrangement in the same way as its big brother above. Bring colour into the display — here red and yellow Achillea are used to portray flames below a grey-brown smoke haze of Wheat and Poppy heads.

◁ Modern Mass has become a great favourite with some floral decorators. It is a deceptively simple display. A large basket or urn is filled with stems of a single species — Lavender and Birch twigs are popular examples. Bold and eye-catching, perhaps, but is it an 'arrangement'? You must decide.

The Dining Room

The dining room is an area which is often chosen for displaying a flower arrangement. The central feature, the dining table, is not in use for much of the day or for days on end, and looks quite bare without some form of central decoration. There is a wide choice — a pair of candlesticks, a bowl of fruit and so forth, but the favourite choice in countless homes is a floral display. There are fresh flowers and foliage during the growing season and a collection of dried or artificial material in autumn and winter. Height and width of the display are usually governed by the size of the room and table — a small Biedermeier arrangement in the modest room or a silver-housed lavish arrangement in the grand home. There is an additional fact to consider when deciding on the size of a dining table arrangement — you will have to keep it fairly compact and light if it is to be removed from the table when a meal is served.

Flowers on the table reduce the bare look associated with many dining rooms, and so does a display on the sideboard. There should be some plant material link between the two but they should not be identical, as their location is quite different. The table display will usually be seen from every angle and here an all-round arrangement (see page 19) is necessary, whereas a facing arrangement is chosen for space-saving reasons for the sideboard. A number of guidelines have evolved over the years. If the table is small enough to allow conversation across its width then the arrangement must be low enough to allow the talkers to see each other — 1 ft (30 cm) is the recommended maximum height for the display. Make sure that fresh displays are pest-free and dried or artificial ones are dust-free. Round arrangements are usually chosen for round tables and oblong arrangements for long rectangular tables, but this is not a hard-and-fast rule.

The remarks so far have concerned the dining room when used for the family. It is, however, a place which is widely used for entertaining (and impressing) friends, and when so employed it offers scope for more eye-catching arrangements. A number of ideas for dinner party displays are described and illustrated on pages 78–79.

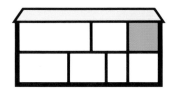

The Bathroom

A display of cut flowers in the bathroom is much more likely to be seen in a magazine than in the home — its lack of popular appeal as a place for floral arrangements is due to two basic features which are shared with the kitchen. The bathroom is generally considered as a utility area so that much thought goes into the functional furnishing (bath, vanity unit, mirrors etc) but much less into purely decorative items. Furthermore the moist atmosphere makes it a poor home for many dried flowers — large blooms with papery petals tend to rot under such conditions.

Despite all this, few other areas in the home need the colours and variety of shapes of a flower arrangement more than the typical bathroom — often a somewhat colourless place dominated by geometric shapes and hard surfaces. Although a couple of features are shared with the kitchen, as stated above, the approach to the display should be different. The casual arrangement belongs in the kitchen — here you can be more dramatic. The bathroom is a place where you can afford to be experimental and have displays which might not appeal to everyone — Abstract, Free-style and the rest. Interior decorators recommend eye-catching containers — silvery metal or shining glass.

As always fresh flower arrangements are best, with an artificial floral display if you want permanence. Dried flowers can be used, but you should choose the ones which do not mind moisture in the air as long as there are periods of dryness in between. The best known examples are Statice, Lavender, Helichrysum and glycerine-preserved foliage.

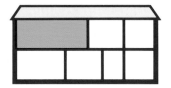

The Bedroom

As with any other room in the house, flowers will brighten up a bedroom. However, it seems that our attitude to having floral arrangements in the bedrooms is somewhat complex. In the family bedrooms the displays tend to be made with dried or artificial material rather than fresh blooms, and there is no general agreement why this should be. Some interior decorators feel that bedrooms are in use for too short a time during the waking hours to make a display lasting for only a week worthwhile. Also when the children are still at home having to top up the containers in several rooms just prolongs the time spent on housework. Finally, there are people who still believe the old wives' tale that flowers are unhealthy in a bedroom.

Things are different with the guest bedroom. When people come to stay it is quite common practice to place a simple arrangement of fresh flowers on the dressing table or bedside table. It is always regarded as a thoughtful touch, and perhaps we like the idea of our visitors admiring our handiwork. Avoid heavily-scented flowers such as Hyacinth and Jasmine, and keep the designs simple. Choose rather delicate blooms — Sweet Peas rather than Peonies and Primroses rather than Lilies. Many experts stress that the colours should be restful and favour the blues, mauves, creams etc. It is hard to see why this should be — cheery colours to brighten the room are quite acceptable as the visitor gets ready for bed, and when the lights are off a gaily-coloured arrangement cannot keep him or her awake.

It is a good idea to encourage young children to make their own flower arrangement (be careful not to interfere more than necessary!) and then take it to their room to admire and care for. Many a person caught the flower arranging bug as a result of this early encouragement.

CHAPTER 8
ARRANGEMENTS FOR SPECIAL OCCASIONS

There are many special days throughout the year which call for flowers. Some of them are national or international festivals or holidays shared by most of the population — examples include Christmas, Easter, Valentine's Day, Thanksgiving and Mother's Day. Others are personal, such as birthdays, anniversaries, weddings and births.

Flowers, then, are a feature of important occasions and have been so for thousands of years. The plant material is generally grouped together as an arrangement, and there are three types of person who are responsible for creating these special-occasion arrangements. First of all, there is the **committed flower arranger** who buys or cuts from the garden the plant material and makes a suitable display. Here we find the table centrepiece of fresh flowers for a dinner party — few people would go out and buy a ready-made arrangement for this purpose. Also included here are the tied bunch of flowers taken to a friend in hospital and the display of bright spring flowers to brighten up the home over the Easter holidays.

Secondly there is the **florist** who is paid to create an arrangement for a client. We rely on the professional to provide an arrangement for a distant friend or relative through organisations such as Interflora and Teleflorist, and it is the florist's job to make a funeral wreath when the sad occasion arises. The floral decorations for a wedding are usually left to the professional.

These first two groups of special-occasion arrangers choose the plant material for themselves. Mintel surveys, however, have revealed that in the 1980s and 1990s almost two-thirds of the population bought cut flowers only when they wanted to give them to someone else as a gift for a special occasion. This means that many arrangements for special occasions are made by **uncommitted flower arrangers**. These people do not choose the type and number of flowers for themselves — the gift bunch is unwrapped and the flowers are popped into a vase filled with water. The resulting display is a reminder of the kindness of a friend or relative rather than an artistic arrangement made by the recipient. To these millions of 'instant' flower arrangers this book is dedicated. The section on conditioning reveals how to extend the vase-life of the blooms in such a display — the chapters on designing and making the arrangement show how to turn gift flowers into an attractive display.

It is traditional to place the red Roses received on Valentine's Day into a vase without other plants — a display of unadorned affection. A carefully-arranged bouquet delivered by the florist may also be treated in the same way, but in most cases it is better to regard the bunch of flowers you have received as plant material for an arrangement. The florist bouquet is usually made up of large and showy blooms. It is a good idea to gather line and filler material (see page 14) from the garden and then make up one of the many styles described in Chapter 3. You will often find that you have enough plant material for more than one arrangement.

As stated in the opening paragraph, there are a number of occasions during the year when floral decorations are an important part of the day. Whether you are skilled and buy or gather your own flowers, or unskilled with blooms delivered with a card to the door, there is an arrangement to make. Ideas for Dinner Parties, Weddings and Christmas are dealt with later in this chapter, but these are not the only times for special displays. As described earlier Valentine's Day is the traditional time for a display of red Roses, but an attractive alternative is to fill a heart-shaped basket or cover a block of heart-shaped floral foam with dried or fresh flowers. Easter is the time for white, yellow and blue displays — here you will have to buy or gather your own Daffodils, Bluebells, Primroses etc as giving flowers is not part of our Easter tradition. Mother's Day is different — the best form of arrangement here is a tied bunch, however simple, made with love and handed over in gratitude by the offspring. The Harvest Festival is an excellent time to make a dried arrangement of flowers, leaves and fruit in red, brown and gold. Church Decoration is an interesting and enjoyable part of the flower arranging scene — do buy one of the excellent books on the subject if you decide to join the flower rota.

For all arrangers, making a display for a special occasion is unashamedly a chance to show off their skills. Choose good-quality and eye-catching material, and be a little more adventurous than when making an everyday arrangement.

Dinner Parties

Friends for dinner. This is obviously a time to demonstrate your culinary ability and it is not an occasion for a simple family meal. It is also an opportunity to demonstrate your ability as a flower arranger by producing a display which is more eye-catching than a simple everyday arrangement. The centrepiece of fresh flowers on the table will be on view from before the first course until after the coffee cups have been emptied. There is no other situation where your floral handiwork will be so closely studied for so long.

No one realised this more than the Victorians — ornate silver epergnes bore lavish arrangements along the length of the table and leafy swags were festooned around the edges. They went too far for modern tastes, but the dinner table remains a key place for the special-occasion arrangement.

This display must be in keeping with the situation. For an informal dinner with a few friends a Biedermeier (page 21) or a restrained Horizontal arrangement is a good choice — flower-heads floating in a shallow dish of water is an unusual but long-established arrangement. Don't assume that varied colours are always necessary — a mono-chromatic display (page 42) can be most effective.

The arrangement for the formal dinner party is covered by a different set of rules. Here the use of candles is highly desirable, and you may need more than one arrangement if the table is a long one. These separate arrangements may be joined by lengths of leafy material such as Ivy, but don't overdo it — no more than 15–20 per cent of the surface of the table should be covered by plant material. Pick up one or more of the colours of the crockery and/or tablecloth in the flowers you choose for the arrangement, and remember that some unusual and exotic flowers provide a talking point.

Keep the display under 1 ft (30 cm) high to allow conversation across the table. The Biedermeier, Horizontal, Inverted crescent and low Traditional mass are popular styles — Line arrangements can be more than 1 ft tall, but they must still be in scale with the surroundings.

A display is often made for the sideboard in which some of the flowers and/or features of the table arrangement are used. Fruit is sometimes included in these sideboard displays.

◁ *A clever use of flowers for the table. There is a central display of red Roses and Ivy — in front of each setting is a smaller version in which just three Roses are used, and on each side plate there is a single bloom.*

Foliage trails spreading out from a central floral ▷ display were a popular feature of Victorian table decoration for large dinner parties. This type of arrangement has all but disappeared, although as illustrated here it can be quite novel and eye-catching.

◁ *The buffet table arrangement is not subject to the height restrictions of the dining table centrepiece. This Mass arrangement adds colour to the crisps, sausages and popcorn, and the coloured pencils provide an amusing touch.*

Weddings

Flowers are an important feature of the wedding celebration both in the church and at the reception afterwards. If you are an experienced and able flower arranger you may well be tempted to make all the arrangements yourself for a family wedding, or you may be asked by friends to take on the task as you are 'good with flowers'. Take care. A great deal of work is involved and people unused to buying and arranging flowers have little idea about the cost and time needed. You will certainly need assistance if you plan to do all the jobs listed below. Most people leave all the floral decorations to an experienced florist — there is enough tension and last-minute things to do without having to make flower arrangements. There is a middle course. Many keen flower arrangers with a wedding in the family feel that they should play some part in the floral scene. So they sensibly choose to do some or all of the more straightforward displays and leave the fiddly ones requiring wiring, binding etc to the professional florist.

There are three major types of wedding arrangements. First of all you will need the personal flowers, including the bride's bouquet, which may be a long and showy shower or a simple posy, and the baskets or posies for the bridesmaids. Circlets or half-circlets may be required for their hair, and the groom and some of the guests will need buttonholes. As a general rule it is best to use a florist to provide personal flowers.

The church floral display can be created by you or the ladies on the flower rota or left to a florist. If you propose to do the work, then it will be necessary to check with both the clergy and the ladies on the rota. They will tell you the areas which can be decorated, the rules about access, the availability of pedestals and vases, the locality of taps and so on. Where money is limited it will be necessary to restrict displays to the key areas, but do remember that the garden and countryside are sources of excellent material — Lilies and Carnations from the florist are desirable but not essential. The most important spot is the side of the altar where the ceremony takes place — here you will need a pedestal display. Another important site for a large arrangement is close to the entrance door — both these key displays should be bold with a simple outline. The amount of floral decoration placed in other parts of the church depends on the money and time available — a fully-dressed church calls for a low arrangement on the altar, garlands around the pillars and the pulpit, pew ends (page 10) filled with flowers, swags along the window ledges and an attractive arrangement in the vestry.

After the personal and church arrangements come the displays at the reception. It is necessary here to keep the main displays as elevated as possible so that they can be seen when the room is crowded. Pedestal arrangements, garlands around marquee poles, swags on walls and hanging baskets or balls above the tables are all widely used. If the reception is held at the bride's home or in a hired hall then there should be no problem in making satisfactory floral displays without calling in a professional, but do remember that there will be no space for large or wide-spreading displays. The situation is less straightforward with a reception in a hotel — you must check that the management will allow you to decorate the room.

It is extremely satisfying to arrange some of the wedding flowers — it may be the only occasion when so many people will see your handiwork. To be successful it is essential to remember that there are several basic differences between everyday arrangements and the displays for a wedding. Firstly there is the maturity of the flowers. For an everyday arrangement extended vase-life is important, so blooms are used before they are fully open. For a wedding you want flowers at their peak for a one-day display, so that means buying flowers from the florist a couple of days before the big event. Another difference is that short-life blooms such as Forget-me-not, Magnolia and Hyacinth can be cut from the garden for wedding-day displays, whereas they are disappointing in ordinary arrangements where vase-life is important. Pastel colours are generally preferred to strong or dark ones, and white or cream blooms are nearly always included. It is traditional but not essential to pick up the colours of the bride's bouquet in the church and the reception flowers. Style is a matter of personal taste, but for most people the traditional type of arrangement is preferred to the Line and Abstract displays chosen by some of the fashionable set.

◁ There may be a large pedestal display at the altar and at the entrance, but it is the pew end display which provides most of the floral colour. Of course this means a large number of individual arrangements, but do not feel you have to spend a fortune — Ivy, a few Carnations or Roses and some garden flowers can look stunning.

Space is usually a problem when the reception is held at home, and so there may be no room for displays on tables and sideboards. In the photograph the arrangements have been placed on the walls and down the stairs — colour without clutter. ▷

◁ Now for something different. The Rose/Ivy/Gypsophila bedecked rustic arch has been set between the front rows of pews and the aisle has been strewn with Rose petals. Not for everyone, and you will certainly need to ask permission before undertaking such a venture.

Christmas

One of the joys of Christmas is the sight of seasonal flower decorations around the house — a welcoming door ring at the entrance, swags and side table arrangements in the hall and a variety of displays in the living room. 'Flower arrangements' is perhaps a misleading term for these Christmas plant decorations as it is foliage and not flowers which dominate them. The big three foliage plants which form the basis for so many Christmas displays are Holly, Ivy and Conifers (Fir, Spruce, Pine, Yew and Tsuga). Other leafy material includes Elaeagnus, Rosemary and Bay.

The purists believe that Christmas is a time for fresh rather than dried and artificial flower arrangements. It is true that Winter Jasmine, Christmas Rose, Anemone, Orchid, Freesia, Winter Sweet and the rest provide excellent material for stunning displays, but the problem is that most people make their plant arrangements before Christmas Eve and want them to last until Twelfth Night in January. Because of this the standard pattern is to use dried and artificial plant material with some long-lasting fresh foliage, berries and cones plus a wide variety of accessories. Glass baubles, bells and ribbons become popular 'flowers' at Christmastime.

The Christmas tree is the centrepiece — real or plastic, it's up to you. Interior designers tell us that several really good displays are better than lots of smaller ones scattered around the house, and a basic theme or a single colour scheme should be present in all of them. Fortunately this advice is generally ignored, as Christmas is a time for fun and excitement rather than good design. Single colour schemes in red, white, gold or silver can look most stylish, but the popular choice is a mixture of colours in which red, green and white are dominant.

Do involve the children — a small dried arrangement with seasonal accessories is easily made by young fingers and is so much more satisfying than sticking paper chains together. Aerosol metallic paints are widely used for adding colour to plants and accessories, but do remember that glitter tends to become detached and then sticks to clothing and furnishings.

For Christmas dinner a wreath of real Holly and Ivy with artificial flowers and candles makes a splendid central feature for the table, but the abundant food, wine, crockery and crackers so often relegate the dining room arrangements to the sideboard or corner table.

◁ *The experts tell us to be less conventional with our Christmas displays, but the holiday season would not be the same if we gave up all traditional Yuletide displays — candles, ribbons and a dominant display of greenery.*

The Christmas Wreath on the door is usually dominated by Holly leaves and berries, but in this one Holly takes a back seat. Gold-edged red ribbon is the main feature, and the prominent plant material is a collection of nuts, fruit, cones and Poppy heads. ▷

◁ *In this Line-mass arrangement the traditional Holly/Ivy/Conifer collection serves as a muted background to a group of single Chrysanthemums. The bright blooms look like glowing lights on a miniature Christmas tree.*

CHAPTER 9

FLOWER ARRANGING AS A HOBBY

It is not the purpose of this book to persuade you to take up flower arranging as a hobby. For most readers it will be a pleasant but only an occasional task whereby attractive displays are produced to brighten up the main rooms of the house or to celebrate a special event. The instructions included here should be sufficient for their needs.

For many others flower arranging is or could be something more — the enjoyment of visiting and competing at shows, watching demonstrations, talking to the experts and constantly trying out new techniques and styles. For them flower arranging is an absorbing hobby, and there are several things apart from reading this book that you will have to do in order to join them.

Read books and magazines on flower arranging

There are probably more books on flower arranging than on any other aspect of gardening. Most are inspirational with a range of fine colour photographs — buy one or two and borrow others from your local library. Magazines are another source of fresh ideas — flower arranging ones, of course, such as *Flora* and *The Flower Arranger*, but also home and women's interest magazines which often show arrangements in room settings.

Look at arrangements in public places

You will find both fresh and dried flower arrangements in a wide variety of public buildings once you start looking for them. Next time you visit a stately home look at the flowers on the tables and sideboards rather than just admiring the silver gilt and the paintings on the walls. Large hotels often have excellent fresh displays and so do large florists and churches, and you can often pick up ideas from the dried flower arrangements in garden centres, department stores and florists.

Attend a course

Reading about flower arranging is both enjoyable and educational, but it cannot take the place of hands-on tuition. At the top end of the scale are the National Diploma courses in floristy if you want to take up flower arranging professionally, and for the keen amateur there are many 1- or 2-year courses offered by private schools and colleges of further education. For the enthusiast with less time to spare the best choice is a day or weekend course or an evening class arranged by the local authority, NAFAS, garden centre or flower club.

Visit the shows

The shows are the highlight of the flower arranging year. The one you go to may be just one of the regular events put on by your flower club or the 'Floral Art' section at the Summer or Autumn Show of the local horticultural society. The standard may not be very high and the exhibits may be modest, but there is often something to learn. Look for material you have never thought of using and groupings of plants which are novel. Town shows and county agricultural shows attract a larger number of exhibitors, and at the forefront are the large horticultural shows such as Southport and Chelsea, and the NAFAS regional and national shows. At the larger shows there are trade stands where you will find containers, mechanics and equipment. Festivals (non-competitive shows) are held in churches and stately homes.

Join a flower club

Your town or village will almost certainly have a horticultural society — other names include 'horticultural association' and 'garden club'. Flower arranging may be included in its range of interests, but its prime activities centre around the plants grown for outdoor display or harvest. For you the group to join is your local flower club — other names include 'floral art club' and 'floral decoration guild'. It will be affiliated to NAFAS (see page 86) and your local library or NAFAS will give you the telephone number of the secretary. The flower club differs in a number of ways from the horticultural society. It generally has fewer members and they are mostly women. Despite its smaller size it usually has a fuller programme of events. A typical flower club will have monthly meetings at which there is a talk or demonstration. Equipment, books and videos are usually available for sale and visits to flower arranging events are arranged.

Exhibiting

You don't have to exhibit in order to be an expert flower arranger. Some people are not competitive and do not like to be judged — others feel inhibited by all the rules and regulations which have to be followed. Do consider the advantages of showing, however, before deciding to be a spectator rather than an entrant at your local town, village, horticultural society or flower club show. Exhibiting teaches you to pay attention to detail and you will receive the honest and impartial opinion of an experienced judge on your skill as a flower arranger. There is the chance of winning an award or commendation, although the prize money is hardly likely to cover your expenses. Still, it is up to you whether to exhibit or not unless you hope to become a judge, teacher or professional arranger — for this latter group the competitive show is an essential part of the training process. As you progress up the show ladder it will be essential to obtain copies of the NAFAS *Handbook of Schedule Definitions* and the *Judges Manual*. Vital reading, but do remember that some organisations such as the Royal Horticultural Society may have slightly different definitions.

BEFORE YOU START

● Choose a local show if you are a beginner. Look at the exhibits at as many shows as you can — read the comment cards and study why the winners were chosen.

● Obtain the show schedule. Read it, and read it again. Study all the details in the schedule — many competitors are disqualified or marked down because they have ignored or misunderstood one of the rules or guidelines. If in doubt, ask the organisers for more information. Select one or two classes to enter — do not go in for too many classes as staging takes far longer than you think. There are two basic types of class. The **Decorative Classes** have always been around, and include such straightforward themes as *Luncheon Table, Swag* and *Miniature*. The **Interpretative Classes** began after World War II and now dominate the schedules. Here you will find such titles as *'Order and Chaos'*, *'Common Market'* and *'Rustle of Spring'*.

● Send off your entry form and fee in good time.

● Think carefully about your exhibit. In the Interpretative Classes the judges will be influenced by originality, so look in dictionaries, books etc for a novel twist. However, there are two points to remember. First of all, don't be too clever — the judges and visitors must be able to see the connection between the class title and the exhibit without having to think too deeply about it. Secondly, this connection must be portrayed by the plant material with assistance from any accessories which are used — you should never use accessories as the prime method of interpretation.

● Make sure that the chosen plant material will be available on the day before the show — put your order into the florist in good time.

● Carry out a dress rehearsal by preparing a mock-up of the arrangement and placing it in the space which will be allowed at the show. It is essential that the display should make good use of the space without exceeding any laid-down size limitations.

ON THE DAY BEFORE THE SHOW

● Condition the plant material — see pages 16–17.

● Get everything ready — make sure that the container, base, accessories etc are clean. Don't plan to take a great deal more plant material than you will actually need. Make a check list. Apart from the obvious bits and pieces remember a flask of coffee, towels, polythene sheeting, watering can and a pen.

● Use a box or basket labelled with your name to hold tools, containers, scissors, mechanics etc. Use cardboard boxes, plastic bags and/or water-filled buckets as appropriate for plant material. Tick off each item on your check list as it is packed.

● Prepare a title card if you have a specific name for the exhibit or if you wish to provide a description.

ON THE DAY OF THE SHOW

● Find the niche or space which has the exhibitor's card with your name or number on it.

● Spread out your material but don't encroach on to your neighbour's space. Use the area under the staging to store your large items of equipment.

● Get to work. First place the drape or background in position, then the base plus container and mechanics. Finally arrange the plant material and accessories.

● Stand back and survey your handiwork. Make sure that all the rules have been followed — is all fresh material standing in water or floral foam?

● Top up the container as necessary. Mist the arrangement but do not mark the background. Place the exhibitor's card and title card (if applicable) in position.

● Tidy up. Look around but do not disturb exhibitors who are still working. Leave before judging starts.

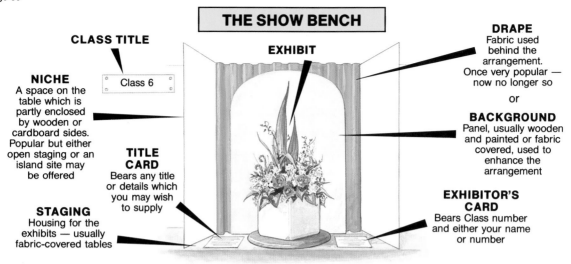

THE SHOW BENCH

CLASS TITLE

EXHIBIT

DRAPE
Fabric used behind the arrangement. Once very popular — now no longer so

or

NICHE
A space on the table which is partly enclosed by wooden or cardboard sides. Popular but either open staging or an island site may be offered

Class 6

BACKGROUND
Panel, usually wooden and painted or fabric covered, used to enhance the arrangement

TITLE CARD
Bears any title or details which you may wish to supply

EXHIBITOR'S CARD
Bears Class number and either your name or number

STAGING
Housing for the exhibits — usually fabric-covered tables

HOW ARRANGEMENTS ARE JUDGED

- **Have the schedule rules and restrictions been followed?** This is the first point considered by the judge, because the exhibit will be disqualified if the schedule has not been followed. Is the exhibit larger than the schedule allows? Are there fresh stems which are not in water or wet foam? Have non-permitted elements (accessories, artificial flowers etc) been included? Any breach of the rules will result in 'N.A.S.' (Not According to Schedule) being written on the card.

- **How well has the class title been interpreted?** The arrangement should clearly fit in with or illustrate the class title — the connection should not be a puzzle. Accessories should not dominate the display nor should they be more important than the plant material in illustrating the theme.

- **How well has the plant material been chosen?** All the material should be in good condition, but it is not a horticultural society show where size and perfection are all-important. Interesting and unusual form and variety are more relevant.

- **Have the rules of good design been followed?** Even a raw beginner will realise that this is an important consideration for the judge. The seven good design features described and illustrated on page 18 are the key areas. Make sure that you follow the organiser's definitions for such terms as Free-style, Abstract etc. At home you may break some of the rules of good design, but follow them on the show bench.

- **How well has the exhibit been presented?** Experienced judges tell us that this point is often overlooked by novice exhibitors. The judge looks at more than the flowers in the arrangement — he or she studies the whole area allocated to you. Is the background scratched? Are mechanics showing? Is lettering on the title card poor?

- **Has the exhibit a vital spark?** As a judge moves from one exhibit to another the phrase "I've seen it all before" often comes to mind. This does not down-grade the arrangements, but for that vital extra point you need an original or distinctive touch.

AFTER THE JUDGING

- See if you have won an award or commendation. Whether you have or not, read the judge's comments carefully and learn for next time.

- Look at the winners and other exhibits — see what the judge had to say about them. Don't be afraid to question the judge if he or she is still present.

NAFAS

The National Association of Flower Arrangement Societies of Great Britain was founded in 1959. From a tiny nucleus of flower arranging groups it grew rapidly and now has about 105,000 members in more than 1400 flower clubs in the U.K and overseas. It is an extremely active organisation — setting standards, holding national and regional competitions, arranging courses on various aspects of flower arranging, publishing leaflets and booklets, training judges and producing *The Flower Arranger* magazine. In 1981 it took the lead and helped to found the World Association of Flower Arrangers. For further information write to NAFAS, 21 Denbigh St, London SW1V 2HF.

◁ *First prize at a National NAFAS Competition was awarded to this Free-style arrangement by Sheila Bishop. Driftwood, fresh flowers and dried plant material are cleverly combined to produce a piece of floral sculpture.*

Sylvana Gianotti was awarded first prize at a ▷ *World Association of Flower Arrangers' Competition for this 'Minerals' arrangement in the exciting Italian style. Two pieces of rose quartz were combined with Phormium leaves, Lily flowers, dried leaf bases and some Cereus stems to produce a piece of Modern Art.*

◁ *An entry in an interpretative class need not rely on accessories to provide the connection. The title here was 'Drought', and this Chelsea entry used dried plants below the floral sun to illustrate quite graphically the effect of water shortage.*

CHAPTER 10

THE ART OF THE EXPERTS

There seems to be general agreement that flower arranging as we know it today in the Western world started in the 1930s. Before that time it was neither a serious craft with its own set of rules nor a recognised art form. Flowers were widely used for indoor decoration, of course, but they were cut from the garden and massed into water-filled containers to brighten the home. The beauty of the display relied upon the blooms themselves rather than the aesthetic appeal of the design.

The history of creative flower arranging in the home is therefore surprisingly recent, but the history of floral art as a whole is much, much older. The first rules for Ikebana were laid down in Japan more than 1000 years ago. In Europe the pattern books of society florists in Edwardian times reveal many beautiful designs including such 'modern' concepts as Line and Parallel arrangements.

What happened in the 1930s was the start of rules and guidelines for the amateur and the first appearance of flower arranging experts on the scene. The first of these experts was Constance Spry, who started her flower arranging school in London in 1935 and in New York in 1937.

There had been well-known names before Mrs Spry. Authors such as Brotherston, Conder, William Robinson etc had written about the use of flowers in the home in the late Victorian and Edwardian era, and Gertrude Jekyll in *Floral Decoration in the House* (1907) had introduced the idea of chicken wire as a mechanic. The work of florists such as Felton, Moyses Stevens and Longman was well known to the rich and famous, but it was Constance Spry who started the first training courses for the non-professional.

The 1940s and 1950s saw the emergence of other pioneers. The Victorian craft of drying flowers was reintroduced and the idea of Line arrangements was brought back by U.S service personnel from Japan. Julia Clements introduced the basic rules for flower arranging to the general public in her 1953 book *101 Ideas for Flower Arrangement*. Violet Stevenson and Sheila Macqueen arrangements were illustrated in popular magazines and the National Association of Flower Arrangement Societies was founded.

Today there are many experts. One or two are best-known for their pioneering work — an example is Marian Aaronson with her Abstract and Free-style designs. Some are known for their books (Malcolm Hillier, George Smith, Pamela Westland, Daphne Vagg etc) and others for their trend-setting style, such as Paula Pryke, Steven Woodhams, Kenneth Turner and so on.

In this chapter there are examples of the work of 14 well-known practical floral artists — the art of the experts. It must be stressed at the outset that there is no suggestion that these are the 'top' 14 — they are a selection of well-known and well-respected practitioners and it is unavoidable that some others of equal merit have had to be omitted. This selection has been drawn from the three types of floral artist — the flower arranger, the florist and the floral decorator. Each of these three groups has its own approach to floral display and each one has a different way of picking out its experts.

First of all, the flower arrangers. This group consists mainly of women and the arrangements are made for the home or for exhibition, but not for sale. The expert here will have won major awards, he or she will be a lecturer and will usually have been a NAFAS office holder. Secondly, the florists. These people are professionals and their approach is different to that of the flower arranger. Part of their trade is to sell plant material and the remaining activity concerns the creation of floral displays. These are generally more stylised than the work of the amateur and the three basic commissions are funerals, weddings and home-delivered displays. The expert here will certainly be nationally known, and will hold a high award from the Society of Floristry. The expert florist is often an experienced lecturer and judge. The floral decorator is also a professional and may also be a florist. The key feature of the floral decorator is that he or she fulfils commissions for creating floral displays in the rooms of large houses, stately homes and public buildings. Here the experts are judged by the quality of their client list as well as the quality of their work.

Look at the work of the 14 experts on the following pages — the brief biographies will clearly indicate the group to which each one belongs. At least three points will strike you. There is no such thing as a 'good' arrangement — the variation is enormous. Masses of material are not vital — some of the greats chose simple designs. Finally, flowers are not the only medium — fruit figures prominently in a few of the displays.

KENNETH TURNER

Kenneth Turner is internationally acclaimed as one of the foremost floral decorators working today. His designs and displays, always innovative and uniquely tailored to their setting, have appeared throughout Europe, the U.S and the Near and Far East, gracing family homes and grand hotels, stately castles and country churches. Born and brought up in Ireland, Kenneth has had a profound love of flowers since childhood.

❝ *A floral decoration should be a celebration of nature, reflecting all its colours, shapes, textures and spontaneous movement. Here I have used my imagination and style to turn garden implements into a master's creation. This 'trophy' sculpture is a symbol of man's relationship with his environment from farm and farmer, garden and gardener — here is how he strives to control and use it. Undecorated the tools look austere and rugged, but with the addition of living plants the image is softened and romanticized. With Fuchsia and fern, Rose and Delphinium, Marguerite and bleached twigs a craft is turned into art.* **❞**

JUDITH DERBY NDSF AIFD FSF

Judith Derby is well-known both nationally and internationally as a professional floral designer, teacher, judge, examiner and demonstrator. She has represented Great Britain twice in the Teleflorist World Cup and in Rome gained 1st place in the Bouquet Section and 2nd place overall. She is a Chelsea medal winner and has created designs for many members of the Royal Family and Heads of State.

" *This interpretation of a waterfall was designed for a dinner party and was placed by the French windows to reflect the floodlit fountain outside. The bell-shaped glass container was filled with imitation Grapes and swirls of Bear Grass to interpret the bubbles in the fountain. Ruscus, Asparagus and Aspidistra foliage provide line material. Lilies give rhythm to the design and Roses add depth and emphasis to the focal area. Solidaster, September Flower, Genista and Bear Grass provide extra contrast in shapes and textures. Viburnum and Elaeagnus picked from the shrubbery link the design to the garden and the Mahonia branch curves above like spray splashed from the rocks below.* **"**

PAULA PRYKE

Paula Pryke has been described as Britain's most original florist. She regards herself as a floral sculptress rather than a floral decorator, choosing where possible natural containers and leaving out mechanics. For her the right combination of colour and texture is more important than the precise placement of material. She is the author of *The New Floral Artist* and has won the Evening Standard London Florist of the Year award.

❝ *This is the kind of arrangement I produce for parties or large functions and it is typical of my style as the container is covered with plant material. Here I have chosen petalless Sunflowers to clothe a round glass fishbowl, using double-sided adhesive tape and a glue gun. The flowers were arranged simply by criss-crossing the stems into the bowl. I spend a lot of time experimenting with colour and deciding what to put together — in this display the richness of the Proteas and Leucadendrons were placed alongside some quite common English plants such as Bells of Ireland and Copper Beech. As always it was my job to match the arrangement to the client's personality, the surroundings and the function.* **❞**

JULIA CLEMENTS OBE VMH

Julia Clements is an international judge, speaker and teacher — her name is synonymous with flower arranging all over the world. She is a Life Vice President of NAFAS and has written more than 20 books. The latest titles are *Flower Arrangements for all Occasions* and *My Life with Flowers*. Although her work has graced such lavish settings as cathedrals and stately homes she still delights in a simple style with a few flowers.

66 *The delicate appearance of these shells brought back from South Africa inspired me to think of a simple decoration using a light container. I chose a round disc of clear plastic, a rose-coloured base, some twigs and a few Roses. An upturned glass was stood on the velvet base and the perspex placed on top. A glass dish holding wet floral foam was then set on the perspex disc and to give height some Willow twigs sprayed with silver paint were inserted. The pink Roses were then added with shorter ones at the back to cover the dish. A string of pearls with more small shells completed the scene.* 99

DAPHNE VAGG

Daphne Vagg is well-known nationally and internationally as a teacher, judge and speaker, and is a NAFAS Associate of Honour. Few can match her knowledge and range of interest from period styles to Free-style and Abstract. A former editor of *The Flower Arranger*, her two latest books *The Flower Arranger's A-Z* and *The NAFAS Flower Arrangement Course* are sought-after 'bibles'.

" *The still life 'breakfast' and 'banquet' pieces of the 17th and 18th century Dutch painters have a great fascination. This group was inspired by them, bringing together fabric, utensils, and the colours, shapes and textures of flowers, foliage, fruit and vegetables. The lighted candle, shell and half-peeled lemon are symbols the painters included to remind the viewer of the worthless vanity and brevity of man's life. The arranger learns much from attempting a more complex arrangement like this. I love its richness, the warm colours, the play of light and shade and the contrasting rough and smooth textures.* "

DEREK BRIDGES

Derek Bridges has demonstrated his art as a floral decorator from Halifax and Australia to Mexico. He was the first man to be awarded 'Best in Show' at a NAFAS National Competition and is also the winner of two gold and two silver medals in World Competitions. His arrangements have adorned St Paul's, York Minster and Westminster Abbey. He has written five books and appeared in three videos.

66 *Flower arrangers do not have to stick to flowers when planning a display. For me anything that Mother Nature produces is there to arrange. Fruits and vegetables have just as much colour, shape, variety and texture but most of all they provide a talking point. A Bamboo table is used to support Pineapples, Oranges, Grapes, Peppers and Tomatoes. The cut surface of the Kiwi fruit was rubbed with lemon juice to preserve it. All the fruit is held in place with wooden skewers. Fruit of this weight needs bold foliage. Cut Fan Palm, Bamboo and Molucella link with the colour of the table — Monstera and Costus leaves complete the grouping.* 99

MICHAEL GOULDING OBE

Michael Goulding has enjoyed a busy and varied career, during which time he has arranged flowers at No.10 Downing Street for Prime Ministers from Harold Macmillan to John Major. Other venues have included York Minster, St James's Palace, many stately homes and hundreds of humbler places. Here is a floral decorator who is a gardener at heart, whose arrangements look as if they have come from the garden rather than a flower shop.

❝ *This arrangement was one of many I have created at No.1 London, Apsley House — the home of the Duke of Wellington. The container was a fibreglass bird bath stood on a marble pedestal; the mechanics were crushed wire netting held in place by wire and with flower tubes on sticks to give added height to the flowers. The foliage included yellow-berried Sorbus, orange-berried Cotoneaster, Stephanandra and trailing stems of Ivy. The flowers were a galaxy of colours with blue Delphiniums, yellow and orange Lilies and Gladioli, white Hydrangeas plus red Gerberas and Euphorbia fulgens. It was a display in the Grand manner, but still dwarfed by the statue of Napoleon.* **❞**

BETTY JONES NDSF

Elizabeth (Betty) Ann Jones has spent her entire working life as a professional florist and is a Past President of the Society of Floristry. Her record as an exhibitor is outstanding — at the Chelsea Flower Show she has won three gold medals and on three occasions has been awarded the trophy for the Best Professional Exhibit. She has no favourite style — she loves them all.

66 *This buffet table arrangement was designed in one of my favourite containers, a Val Spicer candelabra. The three containers were filled with soaked floral foam which was taped down to take the weight of the foliage, fruit and flowers. A colour scheme of peach, apricot, red and burgundy was chosen to complement the cuisine. The foliage included Ivy, Fatsia, dried Strelitzia and Pineapple tops. The fruit (Lychees, Plums, black Grapes, Apples and Pomegranates) complemented the flowers — Anigozanthos, dark red Tulips, miniature Cymbidiums, Anthuriums, Genista and miniature Gerberas. The design was unified by the use of swirling Bear Grass.* **99**

CAROL FIRMSTONE

Carol Firmstone was trained in Art and Design and is a lecturer in Fine Art and the History of Art. A national demonstrator, teacher and judge of Floral Design she travels extensively in Great Britain and abroad. She is particularly noted for her artistic and innovative work. Using plant material as her medium, the craft of flower arranging is elevated to an art form.

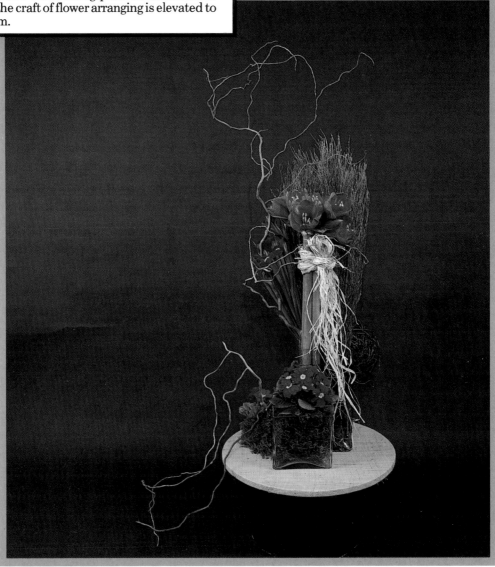

66 *In this piece I have assembled together components chosen for both their individual character and the way in which they work with each other. Smooth glass contrasts with the rough texture of the Broom. Bold splashes of brilliant red are balanced with touches of cool, deep blue. I wanted to make a composition with a strongly vertical feel; the parallel groupings of glass containers, Broom, Amaryllis and Iris helped me to achieve this. The inclusion of softer lines, provided by the raffia, further emphasises the overall severity of shape. Contorted Willow introduces vigorous movement and alleviates the austerity while defining the limits of the design.* **99**

SHIRLEY MONCKTON

Shirley Monckton has been awarded Gold Medals at both Chelsea and the RHS Spring Show, but she prefers festivals to shows. She has designed for events at St James's Palace, Leeds Castle, Hever Castle and St Margaret's Church at Westminster. Her favourite styles are the Plaque, Garland and Swag and she is the author of *Arranging Flowers* and *The Complete Book of Wedding Flowers.*

❝ *This design was inspired by the stone swags seen at the entrance of a stately home. It was made with dried plant materials including gourds, toadstools, conifer cones, lily pods and nuts. The material was painted and then assembled to give the appearance of a stone swag. Swags and plaques are a very enjoyable form of flower arranging and this and similar ideas can be used for decorative work in either fresh or dried materials. It is always an important point to note that the space left within the design is as vital as the space that is filled.* **❞**

EDNA JOHNSON

Mrs Edna Johnson has been a distinguished flower arranger, judge and demonstrator for many years. Her work has been seen in country after country and for decade after decade — Westminster Abbey in 1966, Fontainebleau in 1980, Russia in 1994... Teaching has been a passion, and Edna chaired the NAFAS National Demonstrators' Committee for three years and is an Associate of Honour of the Association.

66 *I am a gardener and my greatest joy is arranging flowers from my own garden. This large display was created for a garden party to make a link between a special occasion and the gifts available from the beds and borders around one's home. The container is a stone statue and is filled with a wide range of the beautiful foliage and flowers available for picking in summer. The foliage display is made up of Jasmine, evergreen Honeysuckle, Escallonia and Stephanandra. A profusion of flower colour is provided by Foxglove, blue Delphinium, Campanula, Alchemilla, Astrantia, Peony, Gypsophila and a selection of Roses.* 99

PAT REEVES NDSF

Pat Reeves is well known both nationally and internationally as a designer, judge, chief examiner and lecturer. She has served as President of the Society of Floristry (1992–1994) and has been a member of its Council since 1979. She was Florist of the Year in 1982, representing the U.K in Germany. She is co-author of the *Naylor Book of Funeral Designs*, a must for all professional florists.

" This intricate wedding cake design is certainly impressive but is simple to make, the mechanics being a Naylor frame with two Oasis mini-decos. The foliages are all garden varieties — Euonymus, Hedera, Pernettya, Euphorbia and variegated Buxus. The flowers are 'Jack Frost' Roses, Convallaria majalis, white Tulips, 'Ballerina' Freesias, 'Cassa' Chrysanthemums, white Dendrobiums and Gypsophila. This wedding cake decoration is designed to grace a separate table at the reception and can be placed anywhere in the room to provide an impressive part of the overall decoration. The purity of the white flowers and the mix of the variegated foliages add to the wedding theme. "

MARIAN AARONSON

Some of the flower arrangers and florists in this chapter work in a variety of styles, but Marian Aaronson is world famous as an innovator in the Modern Manner. She is a lecturer, demonstrator and judge of the Free-style and Abstract arrangement, and is a NAFAS Special Associate of Honour. Marian is the author of *The Art of Flower Arranging, Design with Plant Material* and *Flowers in the Modern Manner.*

❝ *A modern design which relies on restraint for dramatic simplicity. This is maintained by the small variety of plant material used, and presenting this to fully exploit its distinctive aspects. The star performers are the five Strelitzia flowers with their amazing structure and vivid colour combination. Arranged in a lively circular line, they evoke images of exotic birds in flight — Birds of Paradise indeed, as they are popularly called. The rhythm of the design is further enhanced by the vigorous movement created by the loops of Phormium. Preserved Palm leaves, clipped for an interesting linear effect, echo the diagonal thrust of the tallest Strelitzia flower and provide a colour link with the vase along with a strong textural contrast.* **❞**

SHEILA MACQUEEN VMH

Sheila Macqueen has been at the forefront of flower arranging for over half a century. She joined Constance Spry in 1931 and assisted with the flowers for the Queen's wedding and Coronation. She has lectured in many parts of the world including 41 U.S states. Her awards include the Catherine Thomas Carey Medal (Garden Club of America), Associate of Honour (NAFAS) and the Victoria Medal of Honour (RHS).

66 *This mixed green arrangement was created for my own drawing room when the house and garden were opened recently for the National Gardens Scheme. For many years I have tried to get the people to whom I lecture interested in the use of foliage. For me the display in the photograph is a most interesting one, as it was made with a wide range of material and can be arranged at any time of the year. It contains Golden Privet, variegated Ivy, Hosta 'Frances Williams', Arum 'Green Goddess', Phytolacca seed-heads, Fatsia and a number of other green plants. Careful conditioning of stems with new growth is important. Place the cut ends in boiling water before standing in tepid water overnight.* **99**

CHAPTER 11
PLANT MATERIAL DICTIONARY

There is no fundamental reason why a part of any plant may not be cut and taken indoors to be used for floral decoration. With a house plant we demand that it should remain attractive for at least several weeks, but the situation is quite different with material used for flower arranging. Here we regard a life of more than 10 days for a cut flower as a bonus but not as an essential feature.

Some plants which we may wish to use may be poisonous and would therefore have to be handled with care, and others may be strong- or evil-smelling. This rules out a few for general use — many more have no particular charm as material for floral decoration. Even more may look attractive in the garden or in the countryside but very quickly droop when cut. However, even when these non-desirable flowers, leaves and fruits are eliminated from the list we are still left with a vast range of varieties which can be used successfully for creating fresh arrangements in the home.

The purpose of this chapter is to illustrate the great diversity of the material available — cultivated flowers, wild flowers, leaves, stems, moss, fruit, fungi and driftwood. Nearly all of the material we use in practice, however, is either foliage or flowers gathered from the garden or bought from a flower seller. We snip away on our plot or buy a bunch of flowers or two from the florist or supermarket and then we set about making the display. There are scores and scores of books to inspire us with examples of beautiful arrangements and to help us with practical but general advice on conditioning, good design etc. But there is not much information on what we should do with specific plants or what we can expect from them, and there is even less available on the identification of the flowers we buy from the florist.

This is surprising. There are so many A–Z guides to garden flowers and shrubs with beautiful illustrations and instructions, but so few A–Z guides to garden flowers as material for indoor display, with notes on vase-life, drying methods, recommended conditioning techniques and so on. Every garden centre labels each container plant with its name and cultural instructions, but few florists label either their fresh or dried flowers.

The A–Z guide which begins on page 104 is designed to do three jobs. The first one is to list the garden flowers, shrubs and trees which are known to be suitable for arranging, and to provide basic information on them from the flower arranger's point of view. The second job is to include florist flowers in this A–Z guide, bearing in mind that some are commonplace and available everywhere and some others are rarities which you will have to search for or order. The final job is to present a picture gallery of florist flowers and foliage to enable you to put a name to the plant in the bucket or in the bouquet.

KEY

Cutting or Buying stage
This is the recommended stage or stages for cutting in the garden or buying from the florist. It applies only to flowers — fruits and foliage are used when their visual appeal is satisfactory.

- **B**   Bud stage. Some colour but not open
- **O**   Open stage. Some flowers open, others in bud
- **R**   Ripe stage. All flowers fully open

See page 15 for more details

Conditioning method
Virtually all cut material is conditioned by standing in water for several hours before arranging. Some types need a pre-conditioning treatment before conditioning.

- **P1**   Woody stem treatment
- **P2**   Milky sap treatment
- **P3**   Spring bulb treatment
- **P4**   Floppy stem treatment
- **P5**   Large leaf treatment
- **C**   Condition in water for 2–8 hours

See page 17 for details

Vase-life
This is the approximate life expectancy if the plant material is cut at the right stage, conditioned and arranged properly and then given proper after-care.

- **∗**   Less than 6 days
- **∗∗**   6–10 days
- **∗∗∗**   Over 10 days

Preserving methods
- **D1**   Upside-down drying
- **D2**   Upright drying
- **D3**   Flat drying
- **S**   Desiccant
- **G**   Glycerine

See pages 56–59 for details

Latin name	Common name	Cutting or Buying stage	Conditioning method	Vase-life	Preserving methods	Notes
ACACIA	Mimosa, Wattle	O	P1 then C	★★	D1, D2	Woody branches with grey, ferny leaves and small clusters of tiny yellow flowers. Dries well
ACANTHUS	Bear's Breeches	O	P2 then C	★★★	D1, G	A midsummer garden plant with deeply divided leaves and tall spires of hooded purple and white flowers
ACHILLEA	Yarrow	R	P1 then C	★★★	D1, D2	Flat heads of tiny blooms (usually yellow) and feathery foliage appear in summer. A popular dried flower
ACONITUM	Monkshood	O	C	★★	D1	Helmet-like blue or violet flowers on long stalks — leaves are deeply cut. All parts are poisonous
AESCULUS	Horse Chestnut	—	P1 then C	★★★	—	For spring foliage display cut the shoots when the swollen black buds are beginning to open
AGAPANTHUS	African Lily	O	C	★★	—	Trumpet-shaped blooms in ball-like clusters on top of long stems. White ones are available, but blue is the usual colour
ALCHEMILLA	Lady's Mantle	O	C	★★★	D1, G	A favourite plant for use as filler material — sprays of greenish-yellow tiny flowers and downy, lobed foliage
ALLIUM	Ornamental Onion	O	C	★★★	D1, D3 G	Globes of starry flowers — good as a cut flower but not popular. Dry at the seed-head stage
ALSTROEMERIA	Peruvian Lily	O	C	★★★	D1	Not common in gardens, but seen in florists everywhere. Trumpets in many colours. Dry at the seed-head stage
ALTHAEA	Hollyhock	O	C	★★	D1, S	A good choice when you need tall line material. Air-dry floral spikes — use silica-gel for individual blooms
AMARANTHUS	Love-lies-bleeding	R	C	★★★	D1, D2 G	A half-hardy annual with long tassels of red tiny blooms in summer — green-flowered variety available
AMARYLLIS	Belladonna Lily	B	C	★	—	A garden or conservatory plant with trumpet-like blooms on top of thick stalks. Available from florists in autumn
AMMI	Queen Anne's Lace	O	C	★★	—	A good florist flower with airy heads of small white flowers. Available all year, but hard to find
AMMOBIUM	Winged Everlasting	O	C	★★	D1	Not one for the fresh arrangement — a white Daisy-like flower available as dried material. Keeps its colour well
ANAPHALIS	Pearl Everlasting	O	C	★★	D1, D2	An easy-to-grow perennial with silvery leaves and clusters of starry white flowers. Good for drying
ANEMONE	Anemone, Windflower	O	C	★	S	There are several garden types, some long-lasting. The florist one is the Poppy Anemone — not good in floral foam

Achillea

Agapanthus

Alchemilla

Alstroemeria

Latin name	Common name	Cutting or **Buying** stage	Conditioning method	Vase-life	Preserving methods	Notes
ANETHUM	Dill	O	P1 then C	★★	D1	A garden herb — its heads of tiny flowers and feathery foliage look like a yellow version of Queen Anne's Lace
ANIGOZANTHOS	Kangaroo Paw	O	P1 then C	★★★	D1	A conservatory plant with Iris-like leaves and furry flower-heads. Fresh or dry — not easy to find
ANTHEMIS	Chamomile	O	C	★★	D1	Daisy-like flower cut from the garden for fresh arrangements — more often used as a dyed dried flower
ANTHURIUM	Anthurium	R	C	★★★	—	A showy conservatory plant with a straight or curled column-like flower-head above a palette-like bract
ANTIRRHINUM	Snapdragon	O	C	★★	—	An old garden favourite — cut in summer or buy all year round from the florist. Not for drying
AQUILEGIA	Columbine	O	C	★	S	Colourful spurred blooms appear above the ferny foliage in early summer. Grow the McKana hybrids
ARTEMISIA	Wormwood	—	P1 then C	★★★	D1	An excellent choice if you want grey-leaved line material which has feathery foliage. Suitable for drying
ARUM	Cuckoo-pint	—	P5	★★★	—	The leaves of wild and garden Arums are used as filler material. Grow the variegated A. italicum 'Pictum'
ARUNDINARIA	Bamboo	—	P1 then C	★★★	D1, D2 G	The cane-like stems with grassy leaves provide line material for tall arrangements — not often used
ASPARAGUS	Asparagus Fern	—	C	★★★	—	There are several of these 'florist ferns', such as the oval-leaved Smilax and the needle-leaved Emerald Fern
ASTER	Michaelmas Daisy	O	P1 then C	★★	—	Garden blooms in a wide range of colours — most popular types are varieties of A. novi-belgii or A. novae-angliae
ASTER	September Flower	O	C	★★	—	A. ericoides is not common in the garden, but a familiar sight at the florist. Large sprays of tiny white flowers
ASTILBE	False Spiraea	O	P1 then C	★	D1	An herbaceous border plant with large feathery plumes in midsummer. Cut for drying at the seed-head stage
ASTRANTIA	Masterwort	O	C	★★	D1	A drab cottage garden plant — out of favour with gardeners but quite widely used by flower arrangers
AUCUBA	Spotted Laurel	—	P1 then C	★★★	G	The leaves of the variegated varieties of Aucuba are brightly splashed with yellow — winter berries are bright red
AVENA	Oat	R	C	★★	D1, D2	Not often used as fresh material, but widely used in the dried state. Cut and dry when heads are green or brown

Anthurium

Antirrhinum

Asparagus

Aster ericoides

Latin name	Common name	Cutting or **Buying** stage	Conditioning method	Vase-life	Preserving methods	Notes
BALLOTA	Ballota	—	C	★★★	D1, G	A garden plant to grow for its long stems clothed with silvery furry leaves. Preserves well with glycerine method
BANKSIA	Giant Bottlebrush	O	P1 then C	★★★	D1	Hard-to-buy fresh material but freely available as a dried flower. Cone-like flower-head is large and upright
BERBERIS	Barberry	O	P1 then C	★★	—	A useful green- or purple-leaved shrub for line material. Cut in spring for floral display — in autumn for berries. Remove thorns
BERGENIA	Elephant Ear	—	P5	★★★	G	The leathery leaves are excellent filler material for a large display. Available from the garden all year round
BETULA	Birch	—	P1 then C	★★★	D1	Good line material for modern displays — can be used when bare, when coming into leaf and when bearing catkins
BOUVARDIA	Bouvardia	O	P1 then C	★★	—	A house plant available all year round from the florist. Large clusters of tubular flowers — white, pink, orange and red
BRIZA	Quaking Grass	O	—	★★★	D3	An excellent ornamental grass with nodding heads on fine stalks. Use fresh when green or air-dry when ripe
BUDDLEIA	Butterfly Bush	O	P2 then C	★★	—	Well-known garden shrub with tiny flowers in tall cones or round globes. Use as line material in summer arrangements
BUPLEURUM	Bupleurum	O	P1 then C	★★	D1	There is just one species (B. fruticosum) for garden use — florist types are tender. Available as dried material
BUXUS	Box	—	P1 then C	★★★	G	A small-leaved hedging plant — foliage all-green or variegated. Good line material, suitable for small arrangements
CALENDULA	Pot Marigold	O	C	★★	D1, S	Orange-flowered cottage garden annual — modern varieties available in colours ranging from pale cream to deep orange
CALLICARPA	Beauty Berry	—	P1 then C	★★★	—	In winter the bare stems of this garden shrub are clothed with violet or bright purple berries
CALLISTEPHUS	China Aster	O	C	★★★	S	A popular bedding plant with single or double Chrysanthemum-like flowers. There are many different shapes and colours
CALLUNA	Scotch Heather	O	P1 then C	★★	D2, G	White or pink bell-shaped flowers in summer or autumn. Many types have coloured foliage
CAMASSIA	Quamash	O	C	★	S	A bulb for heavy soil and partial shade. Flowering stems appear in summer — 2–3 ft high with starry blooms
CAMELLIA	Camellia	O	P1 then C	★★	G, S	Foliage is oval and glossy — the showy blooms are 2–5 in. (5–12.5 cm) across. Excellent for floating in a shallow dish

Bouvardia

Buxus

Calendula

Callistephus

Latin name	Common name	Cutting or Buying stage	Conditioning method	Vase-life	Preserving methods	Notes
CAMPANULA	Bellflower	O	P2 then C	★★★	—	Star- or bell-shaped blooms in white, blue or lavender. Flowers outdoors in June-August, but can be bought in spring
CANNA	Indian Shot	—	P5	★★	—	This bulb is grown as a bedding plant for its showy blooms, but arrangers use the large bronze or purple leaves
CARTHAMUS	Safflower	O	C	★★	D1	Orange flowers above clustered leaves on tall stems. Rare as a fresh florist flower — popular as a dried flower
CATANANCHE	Cupid's Dart	O	C	★★★	D1, S	A good choice for the flower arranger's garden. The Cornflower-like flowers appear above the greyish grassy leaves in summer
CATTLEYA	Corsage Orchid	R	C	★★★	—	Waxy, beautiful Orchids in a wide range of colours. Best ones are sold with cut ends in water tubes — do not remove
CEANOTHUS	Californian Lilac	O	P1 then C	★★	—	Deciduous and evergreen shrubs which bear heads of tiny fluffy flowers in summer or autumn. Blue is the usual colour
CELOSIA	Celosia	R	P2 then C	★★★	D1	The large and brightly-coloured flower-heads are crested ('cockscomb') or plumed. Available as a florist flower
CENTAUREA	Cornflower	R	C	★	D1, S	A colourful annual for fresh and dried displays. Wiry stems bear sprays of flowers — blue, white, pink, purple or red
CHAENOMELES	Japonica	B or O	P1 then C	★★	—	Red, pink or white blooms appear on this popular garden shrub in spring. For a long display cut at the bud stage
CHEIRANTHUS	Wallflower	O	P1 then C	★★★	S	Grow the ordinary Wallflower for April displays or the Siberian Wallflower for May blooms. The flowers are fragrant
CHELONE	Chelone	O	C	★★	—	An easy-to-grow but unusual perennial for the flower arranger. Penstemon-like pink or purple blooms appear in summer
CHIMONANTHUS	Winter Sweet	O	P1 then C	★★	—	The small flowers borne on the leafless stems are not particularly eye-catching but they are very fragrant
CHOISYA	Mexican Orange	O	P1 then C	★★	G	Cut for its glossy foliage all year round or for its waxy fragrant blooms in spring and again in autumn
CHRYSANTHEMUM CARINATUM	Annual Chrysanthemum	O	C	★★★	S	The blooms of this bedding plant are often boldly zoned in bright colours with a dark central disc. Double varieties are available
CHRYSANTHEMUM FRUTESCENS	Marguerite	O	P1 then C	★	S	An evergreen with divided leaves and multi-flowered stems. Usual type has white florets around a central yellow disc
CHRYSANTHEMUM MAXIMUM	Shasta Daisy	O	P1 then C	★	S	An old favourite in the herbaceous border with flowers borne singly. Usual type has white florets around a central yellow disc

Campanula

Cattleya

Centaurea

Chrysanthemum frutescens

Latin name	Common name	Cutting or Buying stage	Conditioning method	Vase-life	Preserving methods	Notes
CHRYSANTHEMUM X MORIFOLIUM	Florist's Chrysanthemum	O	P1 then C	★★★	S	One of the most popular of all florist flowers — available all year round in a variety of shapes, sizes and colours
CIMICIFUGA	Bugbane	O	P2 then C	★★	—	A large perennial sometimes recommended for flower arranging, but its smell is unpleasant
CIRSIUM	Plumed Thistle	O	P2 then C	★★	S	Several species are offered to gardeners — the florist Cirsium is C. japonicum. Pink powder-puff flowers
CLARKIA	Clarkia	O	C	★★★	D1, S	This hardy annual bears semi-double or double blooms on upright stems in summer. Red, pink, white or purple
CLEMATIS	Clematis	O	P2 then C	★	D1, S	A deciduous or evergreen climber. Attractive trailer for displays, but blooms are short-lived
COBAEA	Cathedral Bell	O	C	★	S	Cobaea is an annual climber, bearing bell-like purple flowers. A useful trailer for the arranger but not easy to grow
CONVALLARIA	Lily of the Valley	O	C	★★	S	An old favourite for indoor display. Small white bells hang from the stems — used to add fragrance to spring displays
CONVOLVULUS	Shrubby Bindweed	—	C	★★	G	The shrub C. cneorum is useful for the flower arranger. It provides a year-round supply of silvery foliage
COREOPSIS	Tickseed	R	C	★★	S	Both the annual and perennial forms of Coreopsis are good for cutting. Flowers are yellow with or without red or brown
CORNUS	Dogwood	O	P1 then C	★★	—	Many uses. There are varieties with coloured bark, variegated leaves, attractive flowers and berries
CORTADERIA	Pampas Grass	R	C	★★★	D2, D3	The largest of the grasses — excellent line material for a grand display. Wear gloves when handling the leaves
CORYLUS	Hazel	R	P1 then C	★★	D1, G	A most useful tree to grow — best is C. avellana 'Contorta' with its twisted branches. Cut and use at the catkin stage
COSMOS	Cosmea	O	C	★★	S	An annual with delicate ferny foliage and large flowers which look like single Dahlias. White, pink and red are the usual colours
COTINUS	Smoke Bush	—	P1 then C	★★	D1	A red- or purple-leaved variety of the Smoke Bush provides attractive foliage material
COTONEASTER	Cotoneaster	—	P1 then C	★★★	D1, G	Many evergreen and deciduous varieties are offered. Cut in autumn for masses of berries and rich foliage colours
CRATAEGUS	Hawthorn	B or O	P1 then C	★	D1	Available from garden and hedgerow. White, pink or red flowers in May or June. For forcing indoors cut at the bud stage

Chrysanthemum x morifolium

Cortaderia

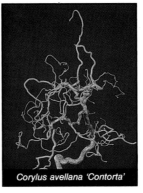

Corylus avellana 'Contorta'

Cotinus

Latin name	Common name	Cutting or Buying stage	Conditioning method	Vase-life	Preserving methods	Notes
CROCOSMIA	Montbretia	O	C	★★	D1, S	Red, orange and yellow blooms on arching stems in late summer. Sword-like leaves are useful as line material
CROCUS	Crocus	B or O	C	★	S	Not a good cut flower unless brought in at the bud stage — the vase-life is brief. Autumn-flowering types are available
CUPRESSUS	Conifer	—	P1 then C	★★★	D1, G	A term loosely applied by flower arrangers to sprigs of any feathery conifer. Conifer cones are quite widely used
CYCLAMEN	Cyclamen	O	C	★★★	—	An excellent but rarely used cut flower to grow in the garden. There are varieties with marbled and silver-zoned leaves
CYMBIDIUM	Cymbidium	R	C	★★★	—	A popular florist Orchid. The usual form is a long flower-head bearing 10–25 blooms. There are miniature varieties
CYNARA	Cardoon, Artichoke	B, O or R	C	★★★	D1, D3	This plant is used in several ways. The shiny grey leaves are good foliage material — the seed-heads are used fresh or dried
CYTISUS	Broom	O or R	P2 then C	★★	D1, G	Whippy branches, tiny leaves and Pea-like flowers. Good line material where a curved shape is required — e.g Inverted crescent
DAHLIA	Dahlia	O	P2 then C	★★	D1, D2 S	Very popular as a garden plant — much less so as a florist flower. Pompon varieties have longest vase-life and dry best
DAPHNE	Daphne	O	P1 then C	★	—	D. mezereum bears masses of fragrant starry flowers on stiff branches in February. Colour is deep pink or white
DELPHINIUM CONSOLIDA	Larkspur	O	C	★★	D1, D2 S	Larkspur looks like a miniature Delphinium with ferny foliage. This garden annual is a popular source of line material
DELPHINIUM ELATUM	Delphinium	O	C	★★	D1, D2 S	This perennial produces bold spikes clothed with large flowers in a wide range of colours
DENDROBIUM	Singapore Orchid	R	C	★★★	—	Each flower-head bears about 10 blooms — many hybrids are available. Usually sold with the cut end in a small water tube
DEUTZIA	Deutzia	O	P1 then C	★★	S	This easy-to-grow garden shrub provides leafy branches with open bells in white, pink, red or mauve in spring or summer
DIANTHUS BARBATUS	Sweet William	O	C	★★★	—	Densely-packed flattened heads of flowers in midsummer — the blooms are single-coloured or distinctly-eyed
DIANTHUS CARYOPHYLLUS	Carnation	O	C	★★★	S	Stems with a single large bloom are 'Standards' — 'Sprays' bear several smaller blooms. Cut stem just above a node
DIANTHUS SPP	Pink	O	C	★★	—	More delicate stems, narrower leaves and smaller flowers than Carnations. Types are Annual, Old-fashioned and Modern

Crocosmia

Dahlia

Delphinium elatum

Dianthus caryophyllus

Latin name	Common name	Cutting or Buying stage	Conditioning method	Vase-life	Preserving methods	Notes
DICENTRA	Bleeding Heart	O	C	★★★	S	An easy-to-grow old favourite — very useful where arching flower stems are needed. D. formosa has feathery foliage
DICTAMNUS	Burning Bush	O	C	★★	G, S	An unusual border perennial which provides tall spikes of fragrant spidery flowers in midsummer
DIGITALIS	Foxglove	O	P2 then C	★★	D1	Well-known garden plant with spires of bell-shaped flowers. Grow 'Foxy' if space is short. Air-dry at the seed-pod stage
DORONICUM	Leopard's Bane	O	P2 then C	★★	—	Bright yellow Daisy-like flowers in spring. It is one of the first border perennial plants to bloom — worth growing
ECHINACEA	Purple Coneflower	O	P2 then C	★★	—	Closely related to Rudbeckia — there is the same prominent cone-like disc, but the petals are pink or purple
ECHINOPS	Globe Thistle	O or R	P1 then C	★★★	D1, G	Round Thistle-like heads on tall stalks — excellent for using fresh or for air-drying. Blue is the usual colour
ELAEAGNUS	Elaeagnus	—	P1 then C	★★★	G	This foliage shrub is a must for the flower arranger's garden. Choose one or more of the varieties with yellow-splashed leaves
EREMURUS	Foxtail Lily	O	P1 then C	★★	—	A garden and florist flower widely used as line material in large arrangements. White, yellow or pink flowers on tall spikes
ERICA	Heather	O	P1 then C	★★	D1, D2 G	Choose carefully and you can have a Heather bed in bloom all year round in white, pink, red or mauve
ERYNGIUM	Sea Holly	O or R	C	★★★	D1, G	A very spiny Thistle-like plant with a metallic blue sheen. Use as fresh or preserved material
ESCALLONIA	Escallonia	O	P1 then C	★★	G, S	The stems of this evergreen are clothed with shiny leaves. The small white, pink or red flowers appear in summer
EUCALYPTUS	Eucalyptus	—	P1 then C	★★★	D1, G	Excellent grey or silvery line material. Maintain supply of juvenile leaves by cutting shrub back each spring
EUONYMUS	Euonymus	—	P1 then C	★★★	G	Deciduous type (Spindle) cut for berries, but evergreen types are much more widely used as year-round variegated foliage
EUPHORBIA	Spurge	O	P2 then C	★★	—	There are a number of garden perennial Spurges which are useful. Stems are leafy — flower-like bracts are red or yellow
EUPHORBIA FULGENS	Scarlet Plume	O	P2 then C	★★	—	A house plant available as a florist flower. The long arching stems are clothed with red, white or yellow 'flowers'
EUPHORBIA MARGINATA	Snow in Summer	—	P2 then C	★★★	—	A half-hardy annual for the garden. It is grown for its attractive white-margined foliage and the white 'flowers' in summer

Elaeagnus

Eremurus

Eucalyptus

Euphorbia fulgens

Latin name	Common name	Cutting or Buying stage	Conditioning method	Vase-life	Preserving methods	Notes
EUSTOMA	Prairie Gentian	O	C	★★★	—	A house plant available as a florist flower. It deserves to be more popular — the blooms appear in clusters
FAGUS	Beech	—	P1 then C	★★★	D3, G	Fresh or preserved leafy branches. Choose from green (Common Beech) or purple (Copper Beech)
FATSIA	Fatsia	—	P5	★★★	D3, G	Grow this one in the garden as a source of really large leaves, deeply lobed and shiny. A variegated Fatsia is available
FERNS	Fern	—	P2 then C	★★	D3, G	Numerous types are used in flower arranging, ranging from filmy Maidenhair to the tough Leather Leaf
FOENICULUM	Fennel	O	C	★★	D1, G	This one is cut from the herb garden rather than the border. Use it for its ferny foliage and tiny yellow flowers
FORSYTHIA	Golden Bell Bush	B or O	P1 then C	★★★	—	Popular garden shrub, flowering in March and April before the leaves appear. Cut earlier for winter blooms indoors
FREESIA	Freesia	O	C	★★	S	A very popular florist flower, available all year round in a wide range of colours. The bell-shaped flowers are single and fragrant
FRITILLARIA IMPERIALIS	Crown Imperial	O	P3 then C	★	—	A centrepiece for a spring arrangement — a group of pendent blooms hang from the leafy crown on the tall stem
FUCHSIA	Fuchsia	O	P1 then C	★	S	Choose a hardy variety for growing in the border — half-hardy ones are bedded out in late spring. Beautiful bell-shaped flowers
GAILLARDIA	Blanket Flower	O	C	★★★	D1	A familiar sight in the herbaceous border — large Daisy-like flowers with red or orange petals tipped with yellow
GARDENIA	Gardenia	O	P1 then C	★	—	A house plant available as a florist flower. Beautiful and fragrant, but vase-life is short. Sometimes floated in a shallow dish
GARRYA	Silk Tassel Bush	O	P1 then C	★★★	G	Long and slender catkins drape the bush in January and February. Cut and arrange fresh in winter or preserve for later use
GENISTA	Broom	O	P1 then C	★★	D1, G	These shrubs have wiry stems, tiny leaves and a mass of yellow, Pea-like flowers in summer. Useful line material
GERBERA	Transvaal Daisy	O	P1 then C	★★★	S	A very popular florist flower, available all year round. The Daisy-like heads are brightly coloured and large or very large
GEUM	Avens	O	C	★	—	An old garden favourite and sometimes used in arrangements, but the blooms hang their heads and vase-life is short
GLADIOLUS	Sword Lily	O	C	★★	S	An excellent cut flower. Remove the top bud. Pick off faded flowers and re-cut stems to prolong vase-life

Freesia

Garrya

Gerbera

Gladiolus

Latin name	Common name	Cutting or Buying stage	Conditioning method	Vase-life	Preserving methods	Notes
GLORIOSA	Glory Lily	O	C	★★	—	A house plant available as a florist flower. The Lily-like flowers are yellow and red with swept-back petals
GODETIA	Godetia	O	C	★★	—	This hardy annual is free-flowering and easy to grow. The gaily-coloured funnel-shaped flowers close up in the dark
GOMPHRENA	Globe Amaranth	O or R	P1 then C	★★	D1	Globular 'everlasting' type — available as a florist flower but best known as dried material. Available in several colours
GRASSES	Grass	O	C	★★★	D1, D3	A number of grasses are used by flower arrangers and some (e.g Briza, Cortaderia and Avena) have individual entries
GYPSOPHILA	Baby's Breath	O	C	★★	D1, D2 S	Very widely used as filler material — loose clusters of tiny white or pale pink flowers on wiry stems. Easy to dry
HAMAMELIS	Witch Hazel	B or O	P1 then C	★	—	Showy, spidery flowers appear on leafless branches between December and late February. The blooms are yellow or orange
HEBE	Woody Veronica	O	P1 then C	★★	G	These evergreen shrubs provide filler material. Some are used for their floral spikes — others for their unusual foliage
HEDERA	Ivy	—	P1 then C	★★★	G	Trailing material cut from the garden or hedgerow. When planting, choose varieties with unusual or variegated leaves
HELENIUM	Sneezewort	O	P1 then C	★★★	S	Easy-to-grow perennials — each Daisy-like bloom has a prominent central disc. Flower colours are yellow, red and brown
HELIANTHUS	Sunflower	O	P1 then C	★★	D3	For giant heads grow the annual type —the perennials have smaller blooms. Dry at the seed-head stage
HELICHRYSUM ANGUSTIFOLIUM	Curry Plant	—	C	★★★	D1, G	Quite different from the popular Straw Flower described below. This one provides grey and feathery foliage material
HELICHRYSUM BRACTEATUM	Straw Flower	O	C	★★★	D1	The most popular of the 'everlasting' flowers — they look like double Daisies with strawy petals
HELICONIA	Lobster Claw	O	C	★★	—	A house plant available as a florist flower. Spectacular blooms in yellow, red or orange — the large bracts are claw-like
HELIPTERUM	Everlasting Flower	O	C	★★★	D1	This annual is often listed as Acroclinum in the seed catalogues. Similar to but less popular than Helichrysum
HELLEBORUS	Hellebore	O	P1 then C	★★	G, S	Included here are the Christmas Rose and Lenten Rose — pink, purple or white in winter or spring. Not good in floral foam
HEMEROCALLIS	Day Lily	O	C	★★	—	Pick or buy when only one or two flowers are open. Each bloom only lasts a single day, so display changes with time

Gypsophila

Hedera

Helianthus

Heliconia

Latin name	Common name	Cutting or Buying stage	Conditioning method	Vase-life	Preserving methods	Notes
HEUCHERA	Coral Flower	O	C	★★	S	Slender stems in summer, bearing dense clusters of tiny bell-shaped flowers. White, coral, pink and red are available
HIBISCUS	Rose of China	B or O	P1 then C	★	—	A house plant occasionally offered as a florist flower. Each bloom lasts for only a day — buds continue to open
HIPPEASTRUM	Amaryllis	O	C	★	—	Large, trumpet-shaped flower. Fill hollow stem with water and plug with cotton wool before arranging
HOSTA	Plantain Lily	O	P5	★★★	D3, G	Pretty flowers, but used mainly as foliage material. Many leaf types available — cream, green, bluish grey and white-edged
HYACINTHUS	Hyacinth	O	P3 then C	★	—	Very fragrant and attractive spring bulbs, but better grown in bowls than cut for flower arrangements
HYDRANGEA	Hydrangea	O	P1 then C	★★	D1, D2 G	Large heads of white, pink or blue florets. 'Mophead' and 'Lacecap' varieties available — see The Flowering Shrub Expert
HYPERICUM	St John's Wort	O	P1 then C	★★	—	Popular garden shrub with large Buttercup-like flowers — some with attractive fruits in autumn
IBERIS	Candytuft	O	C	★★	D1, G S	Annual and perennial types are grown as garden plants. Clusters of white, pink or red flowers. Dry at seed-head stage
ILEX	Holly	—	P1 then C	★★★	G	A great favourite at Christmas, of course, but good line material all year round. Choose variegated types for extra colour
IRIS	Iris	O	C	★		Many varieties, ranging from tiny rockery ones to the tall florist Irises available throughout the year. Popular line material
IXIA	Corn Lily	O	C	★★	—	Garden bulb or florist flower with six-petalled stars on wiry stems. Centre is usually dark red or brown
JASMINUM	Jasmine	O	C	★★	—	There are summer-flowering ones, but it is the Winter Jasmine which is popular. Arching leafless stems and yellow flowers
KALANCHOE	Flaming Katy	O	C	★★	—	A house plant available as a florist flower. Each flower-head is made up of tubular blooms. Many colours available
KALMIA	Kalmia	O	P1 then C	★★	—	Large heads of pink bowl-shaped flowers above Rhododendron-like leaves. Takes several years to reach flowering stage
KERRIA	Jew's Mallow	O	P1 then C	★★	—	Single or double yellow flowers on arching stems. An invasive shrub, so regular cutting for arranging will not harm it
KNIPHOFIA	Red Hot Poker	O	P1 then C	★★	—	Familiar herbaceous perennial which adds brightness and height to summer displays. Red, yellow and orange/red

Hosta

Hydrangea

Ilex

Iris

Latin name	Common name	Cutting or Buying stage	Conditioning method	Vase-life	Preserving methods	Notes
LABURNUM	Golden Rain	O	P1 then C	★	—	Long sprays of yellow Pea-like flowers. Sometimes recommended, but remember all parts are poisonous
LAGURUS	Hare's Tail Grass	O	C	★★★	D3, G	One of the Ornamental Grasses for the arranger's garden. Grow as an annual for the cream-coloured flower-heads
LATHYRUS	Sweet Pea	O	C	★★	S	Lovely flowers on long stems — some but not all varieties are fragrant. Condition in shallow water and keep cool
LAURUS	Bay Laurel	—	P1 then C	★★★	—	Foliage material — the evergreen leaves are oval, glossy and wavy-edged. Often scorched by frost and cold winds
LAVANDULA	Lavender	O	P1 then C	★★★	D1, D2 D3	Used for centuries as a fragrant fresh or dried cut flower. Grey leaves — pale purple, dark purple or white blooms
LAVATERA	Mallow	B or O	C	★★★	S	Annual or perennial garden plant — flower looks like a miniature Hibiscus. Annuals have brighter colours than perennials
LEPTOSPERMUM	New Zealand Tea Tree	O	P1 then C	★★	D2	A florist flower and rather tender garden shrub. The branches bear masses of white, pink or red open flowers in summer
LEUCADENDRON	Silver Tree	O	P1 then C	★★★	D1	Unusual line material — the stems bear silvery foliage and the cone-like flower-heads are yellow, pink or red
LEUCOSPERMUM	Pincushion	O	P1 then C	★★★	D1	This Protea relative bears round flower clusters which have a spiny look — hence the common name
LIATRIS	Gayfeather	O	C	★★	D1	Erect spikes densely clothed with pink or pale purple small fluffy flowers. Flowers open from the tip downwards
LIGUSTRUM	Privet	—	P1 then C	★★★	G	Readily available line material. For added colour choose a variegated or yellow-leaved variety. White flowers in summer
LILIUM	Lily	O	C	★★★	S	Very popular as line or dominant material. Beautiful shapes and beautiful colours. Remove anthers to avoid staining
LIMONIUM	Statice	O or R	C	★★★	D1, D2	Small flowers in a variety of colours — widely used both as fresh and dried material. Very easy to preserve
LONICERA	Honeysuckle	O	C	★	—	Colourful, tubular flowers appear over a long period — fragrant but short-lived. Attractive foliage types are available
LUNARIA	Honesty	O	C	★	D2	Sometimes used as fresh material, but much more often dried at the mature seed-head stage. Pods are disc-like
LUPINUS	Lupin	O	P4 then C	★★	—	Stately spires of Pea-like flowers in many colours. Fill hollow stem with water and plug with cotton wool before arranging

Lathyrus

Liatris

Lilium

Limonium

Latin name	Common name	Cutting or Buying stage	Conditioning method	Vase-life	Preserving methods	Notes
LYSIMACHIA	Loosestrife	O	C	★★	—	Herbaceous perennial or florist flower with tiny yellow or white starry blooms above lance-shaped leaves
MAGNOLIA	Magnolia	B or O	P1 then C	★	G, S	Shrub or tree with beautiful flowers. Preserve flowers in a desiccant — use glycerine for large foliage
MAHONIA	Mahonia	O	P1 then C	★★	G	A dual-purpose shrub grown for its attractive spiny leaves and heads of fragrant yellow flowers in winter or spring
MALUS	Apple	B or O	P1 then C	★★	—	Branches bearing Apple blossom are useful as line material in spring. For forcing, cut at the bud stage
MATTHIOLA	Stock	O	P1 then C	★★	S	Annual or biennial garden plant with small spikes of single or double flowers in white, pink, red, purple or yellow. Good fragrance
MOLUCCELLA	Bells of Ireland	O or R	P2 then C	★★★	D2, G	Rather colourless in the garden but a joy for the flower arranger. Large green floral bells are borne on graceful stems
MONARDA	Bergamot	O	C	★★★	D1	A border perennial for damp soil. The white, pink or red flower-heads are made up of whorls of blooms on upright stems
MUSCARI	Grape Hyacinth	O	P3 then C	★★	S	An excellent choice for Miniature arrangements — the bell-like blooms are clustered at the top of each flower spike
MYOSOTIS	Forget-me-not	O	C	★	—	A popular spring-flowering annual — blue, white or pink varieties are available. Easy to grow, but vase-life is short
NARCISSUS	Daffodil, Narcissus	B, O or R	P3 then C	★	S	Very popular cut flowers. Cutting time depends on type — large singles in bud, doubles when they are fully open
NELUMBO	Lotus	B	C	★	—	An exotic florist flower with large Water-lily blooms and decorative leaves. Cut seed-pods are sold as dried material
NEPETA	Catmint	O	C	★★	D1	Sprays of tubular blue or violet flowers are borne above the grey-green leaves. Crushed foliage is aromatic
NERINE	Guernsey Lily	O	C	★★★	S	A cluster of pink spidery-petalled flowers is carried on top of each leafless stalk. Needs a sheltered spot in the garden
NICOTIANA	Tobacco Plant	O	C	★★	S	Annuals with tall stems and fragrant tubular flowers. Buy a variety which does not close during the day
NIGELLA	Love-in-a Mist	O	C	★★	D1	Multi-petalled flowers half-hidden in finely-cut foliage. Fresh and dried seed-pods more widely used than flowers
OENOTHERA	Evening Primrose	O	P1 then C	★★★	—	Good for cutting — the buds continue to open to give a long flowering period. Poppy-like blooms are large and yellow

Matthiola

Moluccella

Narcissus

Nigella

Latin name	Common name	Cutting or Buying stage	Conditioning method	Vase-life	Preserving methods	Notes
ONCIDIUM	Dancing Lady Orchid	R	C	★★★	—	Small or tiny flowers are borne on long stems which may be erect or arching. Available in many colours
ORIGANUM	Marjoram	O	C	★★★	D1	One from the herb garden rather than the flower border. White, pink or mauve flowers and fragrant small leaves
ORNITHOGALUM	Star of Bethlehem	O	P3 then C	★★	S	Also known as Chincherinchee. Starry white flowers are borne in sprays, ball-like heads or spikes
PAEONIA	Paeony	O	P1 then C	★★	D1, S	Large bowls of petals — single, semi-double or double in a wide range of colours. Perennial or deciduous shrub
PAPAVER	Poppy	B or O	P2 then C	★	D1, G	Cut these papery-bloom plants when the buds are showing colour. Main use of Poppies is as dried seed-heads
PAPHIOPEDILUM	Slipper Orchid	R	C	★★★	—	Waxy, beautiful Orchid borne singly on the stem. Best ones sold with cut ends in water tubes — do not remove
PELARGONIUM	Geranium	O	C	★	—	Cut from the garden when the first flowers are opening. Highly-coloured Zonal Geranium leaves are useful filler material
PENSTEMON	Penstemon	O	P1 then C	★	S	Attractive tubular flowers are clustered on erect stems — the leaves are glossy. Too short-lived for general use
PHALAENOPSIS	Moth Orchid	R	C	★★★	—	Numerous flat-faced Orchids are borne on each arching stem. Best ones sold with cut ends in water tubes
PHILADELPHUS	Mock Orange	O	P1 then C	★★	S	White or creamy-white flowers appear in great profusion on these popular garden shrubs in summer
PHLOMIS	Jerusalem Sage	O	P1 then C	★	D1, G	An unusual plant — the stalkless hooded blooms are bright yellow, and are arranged in whorls along the woolly-leaved stems
PHLOX	Phlox	O	P1 then C	★★	—	The varieties of Phlox bear flat-faced blooms in rounded clusters or tall columns. Many different colours are available
PHORMIUM	New Zealand Flax	—	P5	★★★	—	A perennial grown for its sword-like leaves. This foliage may be self-coloured (green, bronze, purple etc) or striped
PHOTINIA	Photinia	—	P5	★★★	—	Hardy shrubs grown for their oval foliage which is bronze or coppery red when young. The best known is 'Red Robin'
PHYSALIS	Chinese Lantern	R	C	★★★	D1	Flowers are insignificant — this plant is grown for its large lantern-like orange seed-pods. Use fresh or air-dry
PHYSOCARPUS	Nine Bark	O	P1 then C	★★	D1	An unusual shrub for the arranger's garden. The three-lobed leaves are golden, and the flower-heads are dome-shaped

Ornithogalum

Phalaenopsis

Phormium

Physalis

Latin name	Common name	Cutting or Buying stage	Conditioning method	Vase-life	Preserving methods	Notes
PHYSOSTEGIA	Obedient Plant	O	C	★★	—	Tubular flowers on upright spikes. These blooms stay in position if moved — hence the common name
PIERIS	Pieris	O	P1 then C	★★	—	A dual-purpose shrub which is becoming popular. In spring there are bright red new leaves and sprays of white flowers
PITTOSPORUM	Pittosporum	—	P1 then C	★★★	G	This evergreen shrub provides good line material — the black twigs bear shiny leaves with wavy edges
PLATYCODON	Balloon Flower	B or O	P2 then C	★★	S	The buds swell into large, angular balloons before opening out to produce saucer-shaped flowers. Blue is the usual colour
POLIANTHES	Tuberose	O	C	★★★	S	Bulbous plant with grassy leaves and fragrant flowers. The white flowers are trumpet-shaped. Remove the top bud
POLYGONATUM	Solomon's Seal	O	C	★★★	G	Both the oval leaves and the green-tipped white blooms are decorative. These flowers are borne on arching stems
PRIMULA	Polyanthus, Primrose etc	O	C	★★	S	There are many types — see The Flower Expert for details. As a general rule they thrive best in partial shade
PROTEA	Protea	O	P1 then C	★★★	D1, D3	An exotic flower, renowned for its large size and extended vase-life. Usually bought as dried material
PRUNUS	Flowering Cherry	O	P1 then C	★★	S	White or pink blossom appears in spring. The branches may be twiggy or straight, the leaves green or purple
PULMONARIA	Lungwort	O	C	★★	—	An old favourite in the flower border — white-spotted leaves and pale purple flowers. Modern varieties are brighter
PYRACANTHA	Firethorn	—	P1 then C	★★★	—	A large bush or wall shrub which has small glossy leaves on its thorny branches and masses of red or orange berries in autumn
PYRETHRUM	Pyrethrum	O	C	★★	S	A popular plant in the arranger's garden. Large Daisy-like flowers are borne singly on long stalks above feathery foliage
PYRUS	Pear	B or O	P1 then C	★★	G	White blossom in spring. Most interesting foliage type is P. salicifolia pendula with silvery, Willow-like leaves
QUERCUS	Oak	—	P1 then C	★★★	G	Branches of the Common Oak may be used, but the florist forms have deeply-cut leaves and red or brown colouring
RANUNCULUS	Turban Buttercup	O	P2 then C	★★★	D1, S	Brightly-coloured florist flowers which last for a long time in water. Available in a wide range of colours
RESEDA	Mignonette	O or R	C	★★	D1, G	Tiny yellowish flowers are borne in cone-like trusses. This plant is used for its fragrance rather than the floral display

Platycodon

Primula

Protea

Pyrethrum

Latin name	Common name	Cutting or Buying stage	Conditioning method	Vase-life	Preserving methods	Notes
RHEUM	Rhubarb	—	P	★★	—	Young stalks of Rhubarb are sometimes used in arrangements. The curled red foliage is decorative, but also poisonous
RHODODENDRON	Azalea, Rhododendron	B or O	P1 then C	★★	G, S	Azaleas are cut for their flower-heads — Rhododendrons for their flowers and large glossy leaves
RIBES	Flowering Currant	B or O	P1 then C	★★	G	Popular shrub which bears drooping clusters of pink or red flowers in spring. Cut at the bud stage for forcing
ROSA	Rose	O	P1 then C	★★	D1, D2 G, S	The range of garden Roses is vast — the choice of florist Roses is more limited. Cut when buds are just opening
ROSMARINUS	Rosemary	O	P1 then C	★★	D1, G	Useful line material — the long stems bear aromatic grey-green leaves and clusters of blue or white flowers
RUDBECKIA	Coneflower	O	P2 then C	★★★	S	One of the Daisy-like flowers found in the herbaceous border. It is late-flowering — the petals are red, yellow or brown
RUMOHRA	Leather Leaf	—	C	★★★	—	A strange latin name, yet the Leather Leaf fern is one of the basic foliage materials used by many florists
RUSCUS	Butcher's Broom	—	C	★★★	—	Another foliage plant which is popular with florists. The sharp-pointed leaves are really flattened stems. Red or yellow berries
RUTA	Rue	—	P1 then C	★★★	D1	A recommended foliage plant for use as filler material. The ferny leaves are grey-green — a blue-green variety is available
SALIX	Willow	O	P1 then C	★★★	G	A large genus of trees and shrubs used by flower arrangers for the catkins borne by a number of varieties
SALPIGLOSSIS	Painted Tongue	O	C	★	—	The flowers of this bedding plant are eye-catching — each velvety, funnel-shaped bloom is prominently veined
SALVIA	Sage	O	C	★★	D1	All the Salvias can be used as cut flowers — the red annuals, the biennial Clary and the blue perennial S. superba
SAMBUCUS	Elder	—	P5	★★★	—	The foliage of the Common Elder is too plain — choose instead one of the yellow-, purple- or ferny-leaved varieties
SANTOLINA	Lavender Cotton	—	P1 then C	★★★	D1, D2	A good choice if you want silvery plant material with narrow finely-divided leaves. Flowers have little display value
SAPONARIA	Soapwort	O	C	★★	—	A cottage-garden plant occasionally sold by florists. Erect stems bear lance-shaped leaves and pink or white flowers in sprays
SARCOCOCCA	Christmas Box	O	P1 then C	★★★	—	This evergreen shrub is of interest in late winter when the stems are clothed with white-petalled flowers. Strong fragrance

Rosa

Rosmarinus

Rumohra

Ruscus

Latin name	Common name	Cutting or Buying stage	Conditioning method	Vase-life	Preserving methods	Notes
SARRACENIA	Pitcher Plant	R	C	★★	—	Search for or order this one for 'Jungle' interpretation — it is an insect-eater with water-filled 'pitchers'. Truly exotic
SCABIOSA	Scabious	O	P1 then C	★★	D1, S	Flat-faced single or double flowers with ruffled petals. Colour is usually blue but white, lavender and red are available
SCHIZANTHUS	Poor Man's Orchid	O	P2 then C	★	—	This bedding plant bears miniature Orchid-like flowers above ferny leaves. Should be more widely grown and used
SCHIZOSTYLIS	Kaffir Lily	O	P2 then C	★★	—	Rising above the grassy foliage are the flowering spikes which look like miniature Gladioli — pink and red varieties available
SCILLA	Bluebell, Squill	O	P3 then C	★	S	Upright stems above strap-like leaves bear drooping flowers — bells or stars in blue, white, mauve or pink
SEDUM	Stonecrop	O	C	★★★	—	A succulent plant with fleshy leaves and flat heads of tiny flowers. Red and pink are the usual colours. Lasts well in water
SELAGINELLA	Creeping Moss	—	P5	★★★	D1, G	The small ferny leaves of this Victorian favourite are useful in Miniature arrangements
SENECIO	Senecio	—	P1 then C	★★	D1	Grow S. greyi for its densely-felted silvery foliage — the yellow Daisy-like flowers are a bonus. Other species are rather tender
SISYRINCHIUM	Pigroot	O	C	★★★	G	S. striatum is a hardy perennial. The leaves are grassy and cream trumpet-shaped flowers are borne in slender spikes
SKIMMIA	Skimmia	O	P1 then C	★★★	—	In spring there are clusters of tiny white flowers — in autumn the glossy red berries appear and last all winter
SOLIDAGO	Golden Rod	O	C	★★★	D1	Feathery plume-like flower-heads stand above the narrow leaves. Colours range from cream to dark yellow
SOLIDASTER	Solidaster	O	C	★★★	D1	This Solidago x Aster hybrid has tiny yellow Aster-like flowers grouped in plumes like Solidago flower-heads
SORBUS	Mountain Ash	O	P1 then C	★★	G	This tree has several uses — creamy flower clusters in spring, attractive foliage and bright berries in autumn
SPARAXIS	Harlequin Flower	O	C	★★	—	A rather tender bulbous plant which produces starry blooms on wiry stems. Wide range of petal colours
SPATHIPHYLLUM	Peace Lily	R	P1 then C	★★★	—	A house plant available as a florist flower. White Arum-like blooms above large lance-shaped leaves. Miniature varieties available
SPIRAEA	Spiraea	O	P1 then C	★★	S	A large and varied group of popular garden shrubs. White, pink or red flowers are borne in round clusters or long spikes

Schizanthus

Solidago

Solidaster

Spathiphyllum

Latin name	Common name	Cutting or **Buying** stage	Conditioning method	Vase-life	Preserving methods	Notes
STACHYS	Lamb's Ears	—	C	★★★	D1, G	This perennial is grown for its attractive evergreen silvery foliage. The pale purple flowers are of little significance
STACHYURUS	Stachyurus	O	P1 then C	★★	—	A welcome alternative to the ever-popular Witch Hazel and Winter Jasmine as a source of late winter flowers
STAPHYLEA	Bladder Nut	—	P1 then C	★★★	—	An interesting rarity. This shrub produces long bladder-like fruits in late summer and autumn. Not difficult to grow
STEPHANANDRA	Stephanandra	—	P1 then C	★★	G	The zig-zagging shoots of this shrub are recommended by NAFAS as foliage line material. The leaves are deeply lobed
STEPHANOTIS	Wax Flower	O	P2 then C	★	—	A house plant available as a florist flower. Heavily-scented white waxy blooms usually associated with bridal bouquets
STOKESIA	Stokes' Aster	O	P2 then C	★★	S	Something new for the arranger's garden. Blue or white Cornflower-like blooms appear from midsummer to late autumn
STRANVAESIA	Stranvaesia	—	P2 then C	★★	—	Branches are cut in autumn or winter for the bunches of bright red or yellow berries and red-tinged foliage
STRELITZIA	Bird of Paradise	O	C	★★	D2	Large and dramatic flower in green, blue and orange — looking rather like the head of a crested bird. Difficult to preserve
SYMPHORICARPOS	Snowberry	—	P1 then C	★★★	—	Useful trailing material for winter displays. The long slender stems bear marble-like white, pink or purple berries
SYRINGA	Lilac	O	P1 then C	★	S	Masses of tiny flowers are borne in crowded conical spires in colours ranging from white to deepest purple
TAGETES	Marigold, Tagetes	O	C	★★★	S	African Marigold, French Marigold and Tagetes are very popular annuals which last well in water
TANACETUM	Tansy	O	P1 then C	★★★	D1, S	The foliage is ferny and the flowers are tightly packed buttons which look like miniature Chrysanthemums
TELLIMA	Tellima	—	C	★★	G	An uncommon hardy ground cover used as foliage material. T. grandiflora has bronze- and purple-leaved varieties
TELOPEA	Waratah	O	P1 then C	★★	—	This large and exotic flower is sometimes used by floral decorators for showy displays. The globe-shaped bloom is red
THALICTRUM	Meadow Rue	O	C	★★	D1, S	The stems are slender and the dainty leaflets are ferny. The foliage is used and so are the large heads of tiny flowers
THYMUS	Thyme	O	C	★★	D1	A small-leaved herb with green or variegated foliage. Flowers range from white to red — used as filler material

Stephanotis

Strelitzia

Symphoricarpos

Syringa

Latin name	Common name	Cutting or Buying stage	Conditioning method	Vase-life	Preserving methods	Notes
TIARELLA	Foam Flower	O	C	★★	—	A dainty ground cover. The tiny flowers are white and star-like, and the large lobed leaves turn bronze in winter
TILIA	Lime	O	P1 then C	★★	G	Stems of this tree are cut when the ball-like clusters of greenish-yellow flowers appear in midsummer
TILLANDSIA	Air Plant	—	—	★★★	—	The Air Plant most commonly used by arrangers is Spanish Moss. Grey strands used at the base of dried displays
TOLMIEA	Piggyback Plant	—	C	★★	—	A house plant which is fully hardy outdoors. Good trailing material — small plantlets appear at the base of mature leaves
TRACHELIUM	Throatwort	O	C	★★★	—	A florist flower bearing large heads of tiny blooms. The colours available are blue, white and pink. Leaves are oval
TRADESCANTIA	Spiderwort	O	C	★★	—	The herbaceous perennial and not the popular house plant. The silky flowers last for only a day, but buds continue to open
TRICYRTIS	Toad Lily	O	C	★★★	S	An excellent cut flower which is rarely seen. The bell-shaped blooms have dark spots and are borne above grassy leaves
TRITELEIA	Triteleia	O	C	★	—	This blue-flowering bulb is offered by some florists in spring and summer. The flower-head looks like a miniature Agapanthus
TRITICUM	Wheat	R	C	★★★	D1	Not often used fresh, but widely used in the dry state. A good choice where stiff and straight line material is required
TROLLIUS	Globe Flower	O	P2 then C	★★	S	Globular flowers which look like giant Buttercups appear on top of erect stems. Colours range from cream to orange
TROPAEOLUM	Nasturtium	O	P2 then C	★★	—	Widely grown bedding plant which produces masses of yellow, orange or red flowers all summer long
TULIPA	Tulip	B or O	P3, P4 then C	★★	S	Very popular florist flower — cut or buy when buds are showing colour. Longer lasting in water than in floral foam
TYPHA	Reed Mace	R	C	★★	D2	The well-known 'Bulrush' — harvest when the poker-like seed-heads have started to turn brown. Good material for a tall display
VALLOTA	Scarborough Lily	O	C	★	—	A house plant occasionally seen as a florist flower. The red or white bell-like flowers are borne above the sword-like foliage
VANDA	Lei Orchid	R	C	★★★	—	Each horizontal flower-stalk bears 5–10 flat-faced flowers which are waxy and fragrant. Many colours available
VENIDIUM	Monarch of the Veldt	O	C	★★★	S	A half-hardy annual which deserves to be better known. The Sunflower-like blooms have a large black disc

Tolmiea

Tropaeolum

Tulipa

Typha

Latin name	Common name	Cutting or Buying stage	Conditioning method	Vase-life	Preserving methods	Notes
VERBASCUM	Mullein	O	P1 then C	★★★	D1	The tall and stately Mullein provides good line material. The branched spires bear saucer-shaped flowers
VERBENA	Verbena	O	C	★★★	—	A bedding plant which should be more widely used. Small Primrose-like flowers are borne in clusters on top of the stems
VERONICA	Veronica	O	C	★★	S	A florist flower which is available all year round. The narrow pointed spikes bear blue (occasionally white) flowers
VIBURNUM	Viburnum	O	P1 then C	★★	—	A wide range of shrubs grown for their flowers and their berries. The winter or spring flower-heads are usually white
VINCA	Periwinkle	O	C	★★	S	Good trailing material from the garden — both green and variegated foliage varieties are available. Blue, mauve or white flowers
VIOLA	Viola, Pansy	O	C	★	S	Well-known bedding plants which have been used as cut flowers for generations. Enormous colour range
VITIS	Ornamental Vine	—	C	★★	D2	This climber is grown for its lobed foliage which turns golden and then crimson in autumn. Good trailing foliage material
WATSONIA	Watsonia	O	C	★★	—	A florist flower rarity, occasionally seen in floral decorator arrangements. Flower-stalk bears small tubular flowers in two rows
WEIGELA	Weigela	O	P1 then C	★★	S	A popular deciduous garden shrub with green or variegated leaves. Clusters of white, pink or red flowers in late spring
WISTERIA	Wistaria	B or O	P1 then C	★	—	The twining stems are covered with hanging chains of Pea-like flowers. Colours are white, blue, mauve or purple
XERANTHEMUM	Common Immortelle	O or R	C	★★★	D1	One of the 'everlasting' group of annuals. The petals of the Daisy-like flowers are strawy and crisp
XEROPHYLLUM	Bear Grass	—	C	★★★	D1	This modest member of the Lily family is hardly ever mentioned in plant lists, but its grassy leaves are often used by florists
YUCCA	Yucca	—	P5	★★	D	Sword-like leaves sometimes used in Free-style and Abstract arrangements — be careful with the sharp edges and tips
ZANTEDESCHIA	Calla Lily	O	C	★★	—	Upturned trumpets on long stems — upright central column is yellow and the 'petal' colour is white, yellow or pink
ZEA	Maize, Sweet Corn	O	C	★★	D3	Tall grassy plant with swollen seed-heads topped by tassels of silky threads. Ripe fruits (cobs) sometimes used in displays
ZINNIA	Zinnia	O or R	P2 then C	★★	S	The globular or Daisy-like flowers may be single, semi-double or double in white, yellow, orange, red, purple and green

Verbascum

Veronica

Xerophyllum

Zantedeschia

Wild Flowers

Buttercup

In recent years there has been an upsurge in interest in the flowers of the countryside. Seeds are sold for wild flower gardening and arrangers are now using plant material from the countryside on an ever-increasing scale.

There are several reasons for the appeal of the field and hedgerow as a source of plant material. The material is free, of course, but it also extends the floral range and it helps to bring the countryside indoors. However, before you rush out with bags and secateurs it is essential to learn the rules of the countryside. Only cut from plants which are plentiful and never take more than you need — the list below gives examples of wild flowers and trees which are commonly used. Never dig up a plant and never cut a protected species.

With these rules in mind you are now ready to collect flowers from the countryside. Take with you some plastic bags, damp tissues or newspaper together with a few wire ties. The blooms should be cut at the Open stage, when some but not all of the buds are open. Wrap the cut flowers and sprigs of foliage in damp paper and place the bundles in one of the plastic bags. Close the top with a wire tie — it is useful to blow up the bag before closing as delicate plants will not be damaged in an inflated container.

Heather

Cow Parsley

Pussy Willow

Rosebay Willow Herb

Traveller's Joy

Yarrow

BEECH (Fagus sylvatica)
BRACKEN (Pteridium aquilinum)
BROOM (Cytisus scoparius)
BUTTERCUP (Ranunculus spp)
COW PARSLEY (Anthriscus sylvestris)
CUCKOO FLOWER (Cardamine pratensis)
DOCK (Rumex spp)
GARLIC MUSTARD (Alliaria petiolata)
HEATHER (Erica spp)
HOLLY (Ilex aquifolium)
HONEYSUCKLE (Lonicera spp)
HORSE CHESTNUT (Aesculus hippocastanum)
IVY (Hedera spp)
LIME (Tilia spp)
LORDS & LADIES (Arum maculatum)
MARSH MARIGOLD (Caltha palustris)
MAYWEED (Matricaria spp)
PRIVET (Ligustrum spp)
PUSSY WILLOW (Salix caprea)
RAGWORT (Senecio jacobaea)
RUSH (Juncus spp)
TRAVELLER'S JOY (Clematis vitalba)
WILD CARROT (Daucus carota)
WILD OAT (Avena fatua)
WILD ROSE (Rosa spp)
WILLOW HERB (Epilobium spp)
YARROW (Achillea millefolium)

House Plants

Adiantum

Caladium

Lachenalia

In the average house plant collection there is too little flower and foliage material to satisfy the needs of the arranger. The garden and countryside offer a much more abundant supply of free material, and it would be foolish to remove leaves and blooms from house plants in order to provide commonplace flowers or plain foliage. Still, there are two situations where it is worth taking the secateurs or floral scissors to the plants growing in the house or conservatory. Firstly, there are the exotic blooms which do not grow in the garden and there are some house plants which provide excellent foliage. Examples include Begonia rex, Monstera, Aspidistra, Ficus, Codiaeum and Canna. The other situation is the urban apartment which has access to neither garden nor countryside. This means that house plants do have a place in the flower arranging scene, but do not remove material which is in short supply which would have given a much longer display if left on the plants.

Many house plants can be used as a source of blooms and foliage for the arranger — a list of the more successful ones is given below. See The House Plant Expert for illustrations and cultural details.

Begonia rex

Codiaeum

ADIANTUM	FICUS
ANTHURIUM	GLORIOSA
ASPIDISTRA	GREVILLEA
BEGONIA	HEDERA
BOUVARDIA	HIBISCUS
CALADIUM	LACHENALIA
CALATHEA	MONSTERA
CALLISTEMON	PHILODENDRON
CANNA	SAINTPAULIA
CLERODENDRUM	SANSEVIERIA
CLIVIA	SCINDAPSUS
CODIAEUM	SPATHIPHYLLUM
CORDYLINE	STEPHANOTIS
CUPHEA	TOLMIEA
CYPERUS	TRADESCANTIA
DRACAENA	ZEBRINA

Zebrina

Moss

Before the introduction of floral foam **Sphagnum moss** was widely used to hold stems in fresh arrangements. It soaks up water like a sponge and is still occasionally used to fill wire frames for wreaths, balls and cones. **Grey moss** (also known as Lichen, Reindeer moss and Icelandic moss) is silvery-grey or dyed — it is used with dried flower arrangements to cover the mechanics. **Bun moss** is the clump-forming bright green living velvet you find in the garden. It is used to cover the base of both dry and fresh arrangements — it often forms the 'lawn' in Landscape displays. Remember that it is illegal to dig up moss (or any other plant) if you do not have the landowner's permission.

Miscellaneous

Toadstools are occasionally used to add an unusual touch to a fresh arrangement, but they are more often seen as dried material. Bracket fungi are the best ones to preserve — dry slowly in an airing cupboard. **Driftwood** is a general term for any piece of a tree with or without bark which has an attractive shape. The best material will have been naturally weathered by rain or sea. Unweathered driftwood should have all softwood removed and the surface should then be cleaned with a stiff wire brush. Wax the surface with colourless shoe polish. This material is more widely used these days as it fits in so well with Abstract and Free-style arrangements. **Edible Fruit** is sometimes used by the experts in their arrangements.

CHAPTER 12

PLANT INDEX

Acknowledgements

The author wishes to acknowledge the painstaking work of Joan Hessayon, Gill Jackson, Paul Norris, Linda Fensom and Angelina Gibbs.

Grateful acknowledgement is also made for the help received from Norman Allen of NAFAS, Daphne Vagg, Jill Grayston, Asdig Shekerdemian, Beverley Nichols of Jades Flower Design, Flower Council of Holland, Mintel, Britannia Nurseries and Capel Manor Horticultural & Environmental Centre.

The photographs in this book were drawn from many sources. Acknowledgement is made as follows: Arrangement designer/Photographer/Photograph owner or agent (*l* = left, *r* = right, *t* = top, *m* = middle, *b* = bottom) Marian Aaronson/Ken Lauder/Marian Aaronson 64*ml*; Marian Aaronson/Ken Loveday/Marian Aaronson 27*bl*, 64*tr*, 101; Paula Pryke/Kevin Summers/Mitchell Beazley 91; Derek Bridges/Trevor Richards/Derek Bridges 94; Julia Clements OBE VMH/Jon Whitbourne/Julia Clements OBE VMH 92; Judith Derby NDSF AIFD FSF/Stuart L Payne/Judith Derby NDSF AIFD FSF 90; Carol Firmstone/Harry Graham/Carol Firmstone 97; Unknown/Bill Shaw/Floracolour 87*bl*; Unknown/Phil Babb/The Garden Picture Library 82; Erika Craddock/Erika Craddock/The Garden Picture Library 22*tr*, 23*bl*; Michael Pickworth/John Glover/The Garden Picture Library 70; J S Sira/J S Sira/The Garden Picture Library 27*mr*; Unknown/Unknown/The Garden Picture Library 31*bl*, 74, 76, 79*bl*, 81*tl*; Michael Goulding OBE/Sir Geoffrey Shakerley/Michael Goulding OBE 95; St Martin's Flower Club, Jersey/Jill Grayston/Jill Grayston 22*ml*; Sylvana Gianotti/Jill Grayston/Jill Grayston 87*mr*; Unknown/Michael Newton/Robert Harding Picture Library 20; Unknown/ Ellen Rooney/Robert Harding Picture Library 83*mr*; Unknown/James Merrell, IPC Magazines/Robert Harding Syndication 22*br*; Bilton Flowers/Carleton Photographic/HBL 19; Joan Hessayon/Carleton Photographic/HBL 21*br*, 33*mr*, 33*ml*, 34*mr*, 34*bl*, 63*tl*, 63*mr*, 63*bl*, 68*b*, 73*mr*; Gill McGregor/Carleton Photographic/HBL 21*tl*, 21*mr*, 21*ml*, 25*tl*, 25*ml*, 29, 30, 31*tl*, 33*tl*, 34*tr*, 34*ml*; Beverley Nichols of Jades Flower Design/Carleton Photographic/HBL 5, 51, 53, 54, 55, 68*t*; Meikof Kasuya/Ichiyo School Photographer/Ichiyo School of Ikebana 26*tr*; Mrs J Gordon/Unknown/Ichiyo School of Ikebana 25*mr*, 26*br*; Edna Johnson/Ken Nutt/Edna Johnson 99; Betty Jones NDSF/Dudley Button/Betty Jones NDSF 96; Janet Davies/David Lloyd/David Lloyd 41*b*; Sheila Macqueen VMH/Roy Smith/Sheila Macqueen VMH 102; Shirley Monckton/Peter Akers/Shirley Monckton 98; Jo Thirwall/Derick Bonsall/NAFAS 66*br*; Lady Barnard/Michael Brown/NAFAS 41*t*; Sheila Bishop/Harry Graham/ NAFAS 87*tl*; Barbara Boswell/Harry Graham/NAFAS 42*b*; Ann Henriques/Harry Graham/NAFAS 64*br*; Miriam Hill & Zweena Soulsby/Harry Graham/NAFAS 35*mr*; June Lister/Harry Graham/NAFAS 37*tl*; Val Seed/Harry Graham/NAFAS 43*b*; Tunstall Flower Club/Harry Graham/NAFAS 35*tl*; Joan Dunne/Jim Palmer/NAFAS 65*tl*; Sue Brinton/Neil Robinson/NAFAS 83*tl*; Margaret Newman/Saffron Photography/NAFAS 35*bl*; Pamela Howard-Spinks/Rod Sloane/ NAFAS 25*br*; Alverstoke Floral Decoration Society/Jeremy Whitaker/NAFAS 66*ml*; Valerie Ford, Joan Weatherlake & Dennis Barnard/Unknown/NAFAS 33*br*; Pat Reeves NDSF/Studio Bristol/Pat Reeves NDSF 100; Kiyoko Sawada Rudd/Kiyoko Sawada Rudd/Kiyoko Sawada Rudd 26*ml*; Violet Stevenson/Leslie Johns/Harry Smith Horticultural Photographic Collection 31*mr*, 37*mr*, 42*t*, 78, 83*bl*; Kenneth Turner/Clive Bournsell/Kenneth Turner International Ltd 89; Daphne Vagg/D Bonsall/Daphne Vagg 43*t*; Horley Flower Club/John Vagg/Daphne Vagg 36*ml*; Daphne Vagg/John Vagg/Daphne Vagg 24, 32, 36*br*, 93; Henrietta Holroyd/Michael Crocket/Elizabeth Whiting & Associates 23*tl*; Unknown/Rodney Hyett/Elizabeth Whiting & Associates 75; Jane Newdick/Di Lewis/Elizabeth Whiting & Associates 23*mr*; Jane Packer/Di Lewis/Elizabeth Whiting & Associates 28, 37*bl*; Kenneth Turner/Di Lewis/Elizabeth Whiting & Associates 72, 73*bl*; Unknown/Di Lewis/Elizabeth Whiting & Associates 36*tr*, 71, 81*mr*, 81*bl*; Unknown/Neil Lorimer/ Elizabeth Whiting & Associates 27*tl*, 65*mr*; Unknown/Michael Nicholson/Elizabeth Whiting & Associates 79*mr*; Unknown/Victor Watts/Elizabeth Whiting & Associates 79*tl*; Unknown/Unknown/Elizabeth Whiting & Associates 65*bl*. The photographs on pages 104 to 124 inclusive were either supplied by Harry Smith Horticultural Photographic Collection or photographed by Carleton Photographic.

John Dye provided the design work and most of the illustrations for this book. Other artwork was contributed by Evelyn Binns.